职业技能英语系列教材　　总主编　丁国声

English for Civil Aviation Ground Service（Second Edition）

民航地勤英语（第二版）

主　编　◎尹　静
副主编　◎陈　健　刘　颖

北京大学出版社
PEKING UNIVERSITY PRESS

图书在版编目(CIP)数据

民航地勤英语/尹静主编. —2版. —北京：北京大学出版社，2022.1
职业技能英语系列教材
ISBN 978-7-301-31133-2

Ⅰ.①民… Ⅱ.①尹… Ⅲ.①民用航空—地勤人员—英语—高等职业教育—教材 Ⅳ.①F560.9

中国版本图书馆CIP数据核字（2020）第019103号

书　　　名	民航地勤英语（第二版）
	MINHANG DIQIN YINGYU（DI-ER BAN）
著作责任者	尹　静　主编
责 任 编 辑	郝妮娜
标 准 书 号	ISBN 978-7-301-31133-2
出 版 发 行	北京大学出版社
地　　　址	北京市海淀区成府路205号　100871
网　　　址	http://www.pup.cn　新浪微博：@北京大学出版社
编辑部邮箱	pupwaiwen@pup.cn
总编室邮箱	zpup@pup.cn
电　　　话	邮购部 010-62752015　发行部 010-62750672　编辑部 010-62759634
印 刷 者	三河市博文印刷有限公司
经 销 者	新华书店
	787毫米×1092毫米　16开本　13.75印张　436千字
	2008年7月第1版
	2022年1月第2版　2023年12月第2次印刷
定　　　价	48.00元

未经许可，不得以任何方式复制或抄袭本书之部分或全部内容。
版权所有，侵权必究
举报电话：010-62752024　电子邮箱：fd@pup.cn
图书如有印装质量问题，请与出版部联系，电话：010-62756370

总 序

我国高职高专教育的春天来到了。随着国家对高职高专教育重视程度的加深,职业技能教材体系的建设成为了当务之急。高职高专过去沿用和压缩大学本科教材的时代一去不复返了。

语言学家 Harmer 指出:"如果我们希望学生学到的语言是在真实生活中能够使用的语言,那么在教材编写中接受技能和产出技能的培养也应该像在生活中那样有机地结合在一起。"

教改的关键在教师,教师的关键在教材,教材的关键在理念。我们依据《高职高专教育英语课程教学基本要求》的精神和编者做了大量调查,兼承"实用为主,够用为度,学以致用,融类旁通"的原则,历经两年艰辛,为高职高专学生编写了这套专业技能课和实训课的英语教材。

本套教材的内容贴近工作岗位,突出岗位情景英语,是一套职场英语教材,具有很强的实用性、仿真性、职业性,其特色体现在以下几个方面:

1. 开放性

    本套教材在坚持编写理念、原则及体例的前提下,不断增加新的行业或岗位技能英语分册作为教材的延续。

2. 国际性

    本套教材以国内自编为主,以国外引进为辅,取长补短,浑然一体。目前已从德国引进了某些行业的技能英语教材,还将从德国或他国引进优秀教材经过本土化后奉献给广大师生。

3. 职业性

    本套教材是由高职院校教师与行业专家针对具体工作岗位、情景过程共同设计编写。同时注重与行业资格证书相结合。

4. 任务性

    基于完成某岗位工作任务而需要的英语知识和技能是本套教材的由来与初衷。因此,各分册均以任务型练习为主。

5. 实用性

　　本套教材注重基础词汇的复习和专业词汇的补充。适合于在校最后一学期的英语教学，着重培养和训练学生初步具有其日后职业生涯所必需的英语交际能力。

　　本套教材在编写过程中，参考和引用了国内外作者的相关资料，得到了北京大学出版社外语编辑部的倾力相助，在此，一并向他们表示敬意和感谢。由于本套教材是一种创新和尝试，书中瑕疵必定不少，敬请指正。

丁国声

教育部高职高专英语类专业教学指导委员会委员

河北省高校外语教学研究会副会长

秦皇岛外国语职业学院院长

2008年6月

出版说明

英语是国际航空运输业的语言。《民航地勤英语》(第二版)遵循高职英语教学的性质和目标要求,以特定行业岗位"航空地勤服务"为编写内容,注重语言知识技能与行业知识技能的有机整合。本书适合作大中专院校相关专业学生教科书和参考书,也可作为航空公司员工的英语培训教材。

一、编写理念

《民航地勤英语》(第二版)是一本用英语传授民航地勤服务知识的专业英语教程。本教程编写原则旨在使学生在贴近实际工作的情境中,准确地掌握和使用民航地勤服务的各种表达功能,通过语言的大量实践,从而达到能够准确和熟练地运用民航地勤服务英语进行交际的目的。

二、编写框架

本教材共 10 个单元,基本涵盖了地勤服务岗位的各个领域,从订票(Unit 1)到值机(Unit 2)、行李托运(Unit 3)、安检(Unit 4)、机场检查(Unit 5)、特殊旅客服务(Unit 6)到航班非正常运行(Unit 7)、其他服务(Unit 8)、到港后需办理的手续(Unit 9)到最后一单元机场观光、娱乐、购物(Unit 10)。

每一单元都包含以下版块:(1) 导入,看图写话或看图讨论;(2) 背景介绍,每一单元都围绕不同的航线背景展开,都创设了与该单元主题相关的仿真环境下的工作语言情景;(3) 听力练习,每个单元都设计了与主题相关的听力练习,让学生从听的角度进一步熟悉相关语言知识;(4) 每个单元都设有与主题相关的 2—3 个对话,并设计了相关的练习;(5) 单元相关话题或语言功能项强化;(6) 拓展阅读。

三、使用说明

1. **灵活使用教材**　教师可根据学生实际语言基础知识、专业技能、交际能力和岗位熟悉程度等灵活地对教材的内容和编排顺序进行恰当的取舍或调整,可删减部分过难或学生通过自主学习就可处理的教材内容;也可适当增加与岗位密切相关的其他内容的训练,以创造性地使用教材。

2. **强化听说训练**　地勤服务对英语听说技能要求很高,教师使用教材时宜加强对学生听说能力的训练。

3. **灵活安排课时**　本教材每单元按 4 个学时组织内容,整本书要求 40 个学时。但在实际教学中可灵活划分学时,灵活确定教学进程。

4. **注重自主学习**　每个单元中的拓展阅读部分建议学生自主学习。

CONTENTS

Unit 1　Ticket Service ·· 1

Unit 2　Check-in Service ·· 18

Unit 3　Baggage Check-in Service ·· 32

Unit 4　Security Check ·· 51

Unit 5　Associated Examinations in Airport ··· 67

Unit 6　Service for Special Passengers ·· 83

Unit 7　Flight Irregularity ·· 98

Unit 8　Other Services ··· 111

Unit 9　Arrival Passengers' Formalities ··· 128

Unit 10　Touring, Shopping and Entertaining in Airport ································· 144

Vocabulary ·· 158

Keys and Transcripts ·· 163

Appendix ·· 191

Unit 1

Ticket Service

🔹 *Look at the following terms involved in flight-ticket-purchasing. Could you add more?*

Asking for information	Flight ticket reservation	Ticket office
Making a reservation	Round-trip ticket	One/Single-way ticket
Confirming a reservation	International flight ticket	Domestic flight ticket
Canceling a reservation	Time of departure	Regular flight
Purchasing a ticket	**Refunding** one's ticket	**Paying** for the refund
Changing a reservation	**Missing** one's flight	**Rescheduling** one's ticket
Flight number	Business class	A round-trip ticket with return open
First class	**Having** a discount on a round trip	**Putting** someone on the waiting list
Economy class	**Booking** a connecting flight	**Picking** up tickets

Now answer the questions:

1. What information will be required when you are going to book a flight ticket?
2. If you ask for a refund of your ticket within 24 hours, how much do you have to pay?

Suppose you are working in an air-ticket booking office. Your job is to receive telephone calls and offer services on line. Think about your job responsibilities and discuss them with your partner. Here are some useful expressions.

Useful Expressions
Talking about job descriptions and responsibilities ...
The job involves ...
You will be responsible for ...
Offer first-hand information to ...
Make reservations for ...

Dialogue—Domestic Flight 国内航班

Setting: Helen and Jane are Americans. They work at a university as foreign teachers. Christmas is around the corner. They have a ten-day break for the holiday. Jane wants to visit one of her friends at Dali of Yunnan Province during the holiday.

Listen to the following dialogues and fill in the blanks.

Step 1   Telephone Inquiry 电话咨询

Setting: Now she is booking a flight ticket to Dali by telephone.

C(Clerk): Hello. 1_____. Can I help you?

P(Passenger): Yes, I need some information about flights to Dali.

C: Hold on for a second, please. Let me check. Hmm, 2_____.
There are 4 flights on Monday and Tuesday, 2 on the other days. It's very convenient for you to fly there.

P: Yes, I think so. Could you tell me 3_____ on Thursday afternoon?

C: The only flight is CA1849 4_____ on Thursday.

P: By the way, how much is 5_____ to Dali?

C: RMB 1120. May I 6_____ for you?

P: Not now. My travel plans are 7_____. I'll make my reservation later. Thank you for the information.

C: When you are ready to book your flight, please remember Air China. We'll be happy to serve you. Good-bye.

VOCABULARY ASSISTANT

flight number 航班号　　depart 启程,离开　　fare 费用
reservation 预订,预约　　finalize 定稿,定案　　book 预定

Step 2　Telephone Reservation 电话预订

Information Bank

　　flight 航班。每个航班都有航班号。我国国内航班号的编排是由航空公司的两字代码加 4 位数字组成,航空公司代码由民航总局规定公布。例如 CA 代表"中国国际航空公司"、CZ 代表"中国南方航空公司"、MU 代表"中国东方航空公司"、SU 代表"四川航空公司"、FM 代表"上海航空公司"、HU 代表"海南航空公司"、MF 代表"厦门航空公司"、ZH 代表"深圳航空公司"、SC 代表"山东航空公司"。后面四位数字的第一位代表航空公司的基地所在地区,第二位代表航班基地外终点所在地区,其中数字 1 代表华北、2 为西北、3 为华南、4 为西南、5 为华东、6 为东北、8 为厦门、9 为新疆,第三、第四位表示航班的序号,单数表示由基地出发向外飞的航班,双数表示飞回基地的回程航班。以 CA1585 为例,CA 是中国国际航空公司的代码,第一位数字 1 表示华北地区,国航的基地在北京;第二位数字 5 表示华东,烟台属华东地区;后两位 85 为航班序号,末位 5 是单数,表示该航班为去程航班。CA1586 则为国航烟台至北京的回程航班了。再比如 MU5533,上海—烟台航班,MU 为中国东方航空公司的代码,第一位数字 5 表示华东地区,东航的基地在上海;33 为航班序号,单数为去程航班。MU5534 则为东航由烟台飞往上海的回程航班了。国际航班号的编排,是由航空公司代码加 3 位数字组成。第一位数字表示航空公司,后两位为航班序号,与国内航班号相同的是单数为去程,双数为回程。例如 MU508,由东京飞往北京,是中国东方航空公司承运的回程航班。

Read the dialogues with your partner and answer the question below.

Situation A: Space Available 航班座位未满

Setting: Jean calls the Booking Office of Air China to check the seat availability. An agent helps her to book a ticket to Dali next Thursday.

C: Hello, this is the Booking Office of Air China. May I help you?

P: Yes, I plan to fly to Dali next Thursday afternoon. It's rather urgent, I'm afraid.

C: I don't think that should be a problem. We're not too full at this time of the year. Just a moment please and I'll check my computer...Thank you for waiting. Yes, seats are available on CA1849 on December 20th, next Thursday.

P: CA1849 next Thursday suits me all right. I'll book that. Make that a business class seat, please.

C: All right, madame. CA1849 on December 20th, next Thursday, one business class seat from Beijing to Dali.

P: Yes, that's right.

C: Thank you. Would you spell your family name, please?

P: It's C-A-R-V-E-R.

C: Is that "C" as in Charley, "A" as in Apple, "R" as in Robert, "V" as in victor, "E" as in Edward?

P: Yes, that's correct.

C: Thank you. Would you please spell your first name?

P: J-E-A-N.

C: Thank you, Ms. Carver. May I have a telephone number, and where can we contact you?

P: Yes, I'm working in North China Institute of Aerospace Engineering. I stay in 301 of No. 7 Building.

C: Thank you. Is there anything else I can do for you, madame?

P: No, that's all. Thank you.

C: Thank you for flying Air China. Have a nice trip.

Now answer the question:

What kind of questions does the clerk usually ask when someone is calling to book an air ticket?

Unit 1 Ticket Service

Useful Expressions

We're not too full at this time of the year.	每年的这个时候我们的航班都不是满载。
Seats are available.	航班还有座位。
CA1849 next Thursday suits me all right.	下周四国航 1849 最适合我。
Make that a business class seat, please.	请订公务舱。
Have a nice trip.	祝您旅途愉快。

Information Bank

在旅客电话订座中,英语姓名容易听错,为了正确地记录旅客的姓名,旅客报了姓名后,定座员依次读出姓名的一个字母后,再读出字首是该字母的一个英文词,以便核对无误。通常的读法如下:

A	as in Apple	N	as in Nancy
B	as in Boy	O	as in Ocean
C	as in Charley	P	as in Peter
D	as in David	Q	as in Queen
E	as in Edward	R	as in Robert
F	as in Frank	S	as in Sam
G	as in George	T	as in Tom
H	as in Henry	U	as in Uncle
I	as in India	V	as in Victor
J	as in John	W	as in William
K	as in King	X	as in X-ray
L	as in Larry	Y	as in Yellow
M	as in Mary	Z	as in Zebra

Situation B: Space not Available 航班座位已满

Read the dialogue with your partner and finish the exercise below.

Setting: Jean calls the Booking Office of Air China to check the seat availability. But unfortunately the flight is fully booked on that day. The agent puts her on the waiting-list.

C: Hello, this is the Booking Office of Air China. May I help you?

P: Yes, please. I'd like to book an economy class seat from Beijing to Dali on CA1849 on December 20th, next Thursday.

C: Just a moment, please and I'll check my computer...Thank you for waiting. I'm afraid there is not a single seat left on that flight.

P: Not even a first class seat?

C: No, I'm afraid not. We are now in tourist season. At this time of the year, reservations should be made at least two weeks before the flight departure date. However there may be a cancellation between now and the 20th. May I waitlist you on the 20th?

P: What are the chances?

C: I can't say for sure at the moment, but we'll see what we can do for you.

P: Okay, put my name on the waiting-list.

C: Would you spell your name, please?

P: Jean Carver. It's J-E-A-N, and C-A-R-V-E-R.

C: Thank you. Is that "J" as in John, "E" as in Edward, "A" as in Apple, "N" as in Nancy.

P: Yes, that's correct.

C: Thank you, Ms. Carver. May we have your phone number so that we may contact you?

P: I'm working in North China Institute of Aerospace Engineering. I stay in 301 of No. 7 Building.

C: Thank you. If you'd like to make a note, I'll repeat your reservation. I've put your name on the waiting-list for CA1849 on the 20th. When we can reserve a seat on CA1849 on the 20th, we'll call you. Is there anything else I can do for you?

P: No, thank you.

C: Thank you for flying Air China.

Useful Expressions

I'd like to book an economy class seat from Beijing to Dali on CA1849 on December 20th, next Thursday. 我想定一张12月20日北京飞往大理的国航1849的经济舱。

I'm afraid there is not a single seat left on that flight. 那个航班一个座位也没有剩。

We are now in tourist season. 我们正处于旅游旺季。

Reservations should be made at least two weeks before the flight departure date. 要提前两个星期订票。

May I waitlist you on the 20th？ 我可以把您列入20日航班的候补名单吗？

Unit 1 Ticket Service

Match words and translations in the two columns.

1. 预订机票
2. 检查订座情况
3. 列入等候名单
4. 头等舱
5. 到达时间
6. 不要挂电话
7. 最早的航班
8. 经济舱
9. 国内航班
10. 误机乘客
11. 启程时间
12. 公务舱

A. Arrival time
B. Book a flight ticket
C. Departure time
D. Hold on for a moment
E. Economy-class
F. Domestic flight
G. First-class
H. No-shows
I. Business-class
J. Earliest flight
K. Check the availability
L. Put...on the waiting-list

Step 3 Telephone Confirmation 电话确认

Situation A: Confirming the Reservation 确认订座

Setting: Jean has made a reservation for a flight to Dali, and she calls the Booking Office of Air China to confirm her reservation.

C: Hello, this is Air China Booking Office.

P: Hello. I'd like to confirm my flight reservation.

C: May I know your flight number, please?

P: It's flight CA1849, which leaves Beijing at 13:40 on December 20th.

C: Oh, yes. That's our regular flight to Dali. Would you please tell me your name?

P: My name is Jean Carver.

C: Yes, Ms. Carter, here you are. You're flying in first class. Is that right?

P: Oh, no. I'm sure I made a reservation for an economy-class ticket. My name is Carver, not Carter.

C: Let me check. Aha! I've got it. Now, your ticket is in order. Thank you for calling to confirm.

P: It's better to confirm after ordering, right? And I don't want to lose it.

C: Quite right. If you hadn't confirmed, it would be cancelled within 24 hours before the departure time. In order not to miss your flight, I think you should pick up your ticket as early as possible.

P: Okay, I shall.

Information Bank

航班号的一般读法：

CA127	CA one twenty-seven
SH5241	SH fifty-two forty-one
UA05	UA o five

◆ **Make up your own dialogues with your partner according to the following condition.**

You are calling to Airticket Service Office to confirm your flight to Hong Kong with the clerk. Your flight is CZ369 at 13:45 on Monday September 21st.

◆ **Situation B: Cancelling the Reservation 取消订座**

Setting: Jane Carver's reservation from Beijing to Dali has been cancelled because she did not call Air China to confirm her reservation 24 hours before the flight departure. As a result, she has to take a next day flight.

C: Hello, this is Air China Booking Office. How may I help you?

P: Hello. I'm scheduled on your flight CA1849 from Beijing to Dali tomorrow afternoon. I'd like to make sure that there is no problem with my reservation.

C: I'll be happy to check for you. But I need to retrieve your reservation record in my computer first. Could you tell me your last name, please?

P: Carver. It's C-A-R-V-E-R.

...

C: Thank you for waiting, Ms. Carver. Your record shows that your reservation from Beijing to Dali has been cancelled.

P: What? I called your office last week and booked my seat from Beijing to Dali on December 20th, Thursday on CA1849 departing at 13:40 tomorrow.

C: I believe that the cancellation is due to your failure to confirm. You know, passengers are requested to confirm their seats at least 24 hours before the flight departure time. Failure to do that will result in automatic cancellation.

P: Are you trying to tell me that I can't get on the flight tomorrow afternoon?

C: I'm sorry, ma'am. Seats are not available on tomorrow's CA1849.

P: It's too bad that I didn't notice the confirmation rule.

C: I'm sorry. But would you like me to reserve a seat for you to Dali for the day after tomorrow?

P: Do you expect any no-shows for CA1849 tomorrow morning? If so, I'd like to standby at the airport.

Unit 1 Ticket Service

C: I don't think so, ma'am. Your chances are not good.

P: All right, if this is the best you can do for me.

C: Thank you, ma'am. You are confirmed on CA1919 the day after tomorrow, December 21st. It leaves Beijing at 8:40 a.m. and arrives in Dali at 10:25 a.m. May I have your telephone number in Beijing where we can call you?

P: Oh, yes. It's 010-20596882.

C: 010-20596882. Please check in at least 2 hours prior to the flight departure. Is there anything else I can do for you?

P: No, thanks.

C: You are welcome. Thank you for flying Air China.

> **Useful Expressions**
> No-shows: 误机乘客。 Go-shows: 到机场等待的候补旅客。
> Standby: 等待候补。Standby 也可以当名词用，如 There are five standbys for CA753 to Los Angeles. 前往洛杉矶的国航753航班有五名候补旅客。
> I'm scheduled on your flight CA1849 from Beijing to Dali tomorrow afternoon. I'd like to make sure that there is no problem with my reservation. 我预订了明天下午国航CA1849北京到大理的机票，我想确认一下。
> Your record shows that your reservation from Beijing to Dali has been cancelled. 记录显示您北京至大理的预订取消了。

✢ *Complete the following dialogue and practice with your partner.*

(Mr. Brown has reserved a ticket from Beijing back to New York next Monday. But he has an urgent business meeting in Beijing next Tuesday morning, so he has to cancel his reservation.)

C: This is Air China Ticket Office. May I help you?

P: Yes. 1_____.(我订了一张下周一从北京飞往纽约的票。) But I need to stay in Beijing for a couple more days. 2_____.(我不得不取消预订的座位。)

C: 3_____?（请告诉我航班号？）

P: Yes, CA421.

C: 4_____?（您的姓名？）

P: Davie Brown.

C: Hold on, please. Let me check.（A moment later）Oh, 5_____.(找到了。) 6_____.(您预订了下周一9月27日国航CA421航班的头等舱。)

P: That's right.

C: Mr. Brown. I'll cancel your reservation.

9

P: Thank you.
C: 7_____? (您想预订别的航班吗？)
P: No, thank you. I'll call you if I want.
C: 8_____! (感谢来电。布朗先生。再见！)
P: Good-bye.

Make up dialogues for each of the following situations.

(1) Miss Zhao has made a reservation on flight MU5533 to Yantai. She calls the air-ticket booking office to confirm her reservation 2 days before the flight departure.

(2) Mr. Li has made a reservation from Beijing to Xi'an on flight SZ3215. Now his plan has changed and he wants to cancel his reservation.

Dialogue—International Flight 国际航班

Setting: Helen is going to finish her teaching in NCIAE for this semester. So she is planning to fly back to New York in December. So now she is at the booking office trying to book an air ticket.

Step 1 Booking a Ticket 订票

Setting: Helen is not sure about when she could finish her finals. So she is asking for suggestions from the agent.

P: Hello, I want to book a seat to New York. But I'm afraid I don't know when I can leave.
C: How can you book a seat then?
P: Well, that depends on when I could finish my finals for my students. Hopefully I could get them examined before December 15th, so that I could go back to America in time. But I'm not sure until I have the timetable for the finals.
C: When do you think you could have that?
P: I don't know exactly. Generally, I could have that timetable by the end of this month. So may I book a seat for next month right now?
C: All right, miss. What is your name, please?
P: Helen, H-E-L-E-N.
C: There are three flights going to New York every week, Monday, Wednesday and Friday. Which do you prefer, then?
P: I'd like the Monday's flight of the third week in December.
C: Ok, I can make a reservation on flight CA981 on December 16th.
P: Thank you very much.

Setting: Several days later, Helen is coming to the office again. She can't finish her finals until December 21st. So she is rebooking her seat.

P: My name is Helen. I made a reservation for flight CA981 on December 16th last month. But so far I haven't finished my finals yet until December 21st. So I have to make another reservation.

C: On which day do you prefer to go now?

P: Please cancel my last reservation and make a reservation for flight CA939 on December 22nd.

C: Ok, please confirm your reservation when you get your work done.

P: I will.

Information Bank

国内部分航空公司代码

中国国际航空公司	CA	中国东方航空公司	MU
中国西北航空公司	WH	厦门航空有限公司	MF
中国南方航空公司	CZ	上海航空公司	FM
中国西南航空公司	SZ	山东航空公司	SC

国外部分航空公司代码

法国航空公司	AF	澳大利亚快达航空公司	QF
英国航空公司	BA	瑞士航空公司	SU
大韩航空公司	KE	芬兰航空公司	AY
德国汉莎航空公司	LH	日本航空公司	JD
美国西北航空公司	NW	全日空公司	NH
韩亚航空公司	OZ	新加坡航空公司	SQ
美国联合航空公司	UA	荷兰皇家航空公司	KL

Step 2 Purchasing the Ticket 买票

Setting: Helen has got her work done in time and made the reservation by telephone with the office. Now she is coming to pick up the ticket.

P: Hello, I'm coming to pick up my ticket which I've booked already.

C: All right. Could you tell me your name and the flight number?

P: Helen. Flight number is CA939 on December 22nd.

C: Yes, miss. It's RMB 5800. Would you pay in cash or by your credit card?

P: Cash, please.

C: Okay, may I see your passport, please?

P: Of course. Here you are.

C: Thank you. (Hands back the passport.) Here's your ticket. Please check in at the airport no later than 4:00 p.m. that day.

> **Useful Expressions**
> visa 签证   passport 护照
> purchase a ticket 买票   pick up a ticket 取票
> make a reservation 预订(机票、餐桌、酒店客房等)
> pay in cash or with credit card 现金支付或信用卡支付
> Please check in at the airport no later than 4:00 p.m. that day. 请在当天下午四点前办理登记手续。

Step 3 Refunding the Ticket 退票

Setting: One day before Heidi's departure, she changes her plan due to some urgent matters at her school. Now she is at the office desk.

C: Good morning. Anything I can do for you?

P: Good morning, miss. I have bought a ticket on flight CA939, flying to New York at 6:05 p.m. tomorrow. But unfortunately, I have something more important to do and I have to stay here for a few more days. Could you please help me change the date for December 25th and flight number for CA913?

C: I'm sorry to tell you that we can't change any words written on the ticket. According to CAAC's regulations, when a passenger wants to change his flight, date, route or his name to another's, his ticket will be handled as a refund ticket. That is to say, you have to buy another ticket.

P: Oh, I see. Do I have to pay for the refund?

C: Yes, you have to pay RMB580 for the refund.

P: Why should I pay so much? Would you tell me the reason?

C: Yes, miss. According to CAAC's regulation, if a passenger (except a group passenger) asks for a refund of his ticket 24 hours before the departure time, the cancellation fee is 10% of the original fare.

P: What about within 24 hours?

C: If the passenger asks for a refund of his ticket within 24 hours and 2 hours before the departure time, he has to pay 20% of the original fare.

P: If he asks for a refund of his ticket within 2 hours before the departure time, he has to pay much more. Right?

C: Yes, right. The cancellation fee would be 50% of the original fare.

P: Thanks for your information. Here is my ticket and the money for the refund.

C: Here is your receipt.

Unit 1 Ticket Service

Useful Expressions

I'm sorry to tell you that we can't change any words written on the ticket. According to CAAC's regulations, when a passenger wants to change his flight, date, route or his name to another's, his ticket will be handled as a refund ticket. That is to say, you have to buy another ticket.

很抱歉,飞机票上面写的字一个也不能改。根据中国民航的规定,旅客要求变更航班、日期、航线或旅客姓名,该机票则按退票处理。也就是说,您得另外买一张机票。

According to CAAC's regulation, if a passenger (except a group passenger) asks for a refund of his ticket 24 hours before the departure time, the cancellation fee is 10% of the original fare.

根据中国民航规定,如果旅客(不包括团体旅客)在飞机起飞24小时以前申报退票,按原价的10%收取退票费。

If the passenger asks for a refund of his ticket within 24 hours and 2 hours before the departure time, he has to pay 20% of the original fare.

如果旅客在飞机起飞24小时以内,2小时以前申请退票,他得按照原票价的20%交退票费。

If he asks for a refund of his ticket within 2 hours before the departure time, he has to pay much more. The cancellation fee would be 50% of the original fare.

如果在飞机起飞2小时以内申请退票,他得交更多的退票费,为原价的50%。

Information Bank

Ticket Refund 退票

退票分为自愿退票和非自愿退票两类。由于旅客的原因而引起的退票为自愿退票;不是由于旅客原因而引起的退票为非自愿退票。旅客应凭客票或客票未使用部分的"乘机联"和"旅客联"办理退票。

国内航班退票只限在出票地、航班始发地、终止旅行地的航空公司或其销售代理人售票处办理。票款只能退给客票上列明的旅客本人或客票的付款人。

国际航班退票应在原购票地点或者经航空公司同意的其他地点,并符合原购票地点和退票地点国家的法律及其他规定。

自愿退票,除凭有效客票外,还应提供旅客本人的有效身份证件。革命伤残军人和因公致残的人民警察要求退票,免收退票费。持婴儿客票的旅客退票,免收退票费。持不定期客票的旅客要求退票,应在客票的有效期内到原购票地点办理退票手续。旅客在航班的经停地自动终止旅行,该航班未使用航段的票款不退。

因航空公司原因造成航班取消、提前、延误、航程改变或不能提供原订座位时,旅客要求退票,始发站应退还全部票款,经停地应退还未使用航段的全部票款,均不收取退票费。

旅客因病(包括患病旅客的陪伴人员)要求退票,需提供医疗单位的证明,始发地应退还全部票款,经停地应退还未使用航段的全部票款,均不收取退票费。

Answer these questions.

(1) If you want to know which class of service the passenger desires, what would you say?
(2) If space is not available on the flight that the passenger desires, what would you say and suggest to the passenger?
(3) Mr. Green fails to reconfirm his reservation for an international flight within 72 hours before departure and his reservation has been canceled. What should you say to him?
(4) Mr. Williams wants to refund his ticket from Hong Kong to Tokyo 36 hours before the flight's departure. How much he has to pay and how do you say to him?

Complete the following dialogue and practice with your partner.

(Mr. Gabriel has missed the flight CA819 to New York. He goes to the Air China Ticket Office to reschedule his ticket.)

C: 1_____? (您好,有什么事吗?)

P: I just missed my flight due to a traffic jam. Can I reschedule it?

C: 2_____? (可以,您要去哪儿?)

P: New York.

C: 3_____. (CA1314后天上午12:40起飞。)

P: Do you have anything earlier?

C: Let me check. 4_____? (CA542 明天下午15:20起飞,还有空座,签这个航班行吗?)

P: Ok, I'll take that.

C: Let me have your passport and your original ticket, please.

P: 5_____? (给您,顺便问一下,我还要再付费吗?)

C: No, you don't. Here are your ticket and passport.

P: Thank you.

C: 6_____. (谢谢您选择国航的航班。)

➕ Make up your own dialogues with your partner according to the following condition.

Mr. Wright is taking a flight from New York to Chicago. It leaves at four o'clock and arrives at six o'clock. He wants to know whether dinner is served on the flight. If dinner is not served, he wants to change his reservation to a later flight on which dinner will be served.

★ Further Reading 1

The Reservations Agent

Most people want to make their flight reservations by telephoning an airline reservations office. A reservations agent is responsible for making or confirming reservations for passengers who telephone the airline. Before going to reservations control to check whether or not there is a space available, the reservations agent will have to determine what time and day are most desirable for the passengers, find out whether the passenger is traveling alone or with other people and get the name of the passenger. In addition, he must find out which class of service the passenger desires, that is, first class, business or economy class. If space is not available on the flight that the passenger desires, it is advisable that the agent suggests an alternate flight. Besides reservations, a reservations agent is also supposed to give any other information the passenger may need, such as weather conditions and food service.

The main job of a reservations agent is to make a sale—that is, to confirm space on his own airline that is as close as possible to the passenger's needs and desires. However, the airlines receive a large number of calls that do not result in sales. These calls for general information must be handled with the same efficiency and courtesy as calls that end with confirmed reservations. Many passengers consider the voice on the other end of the phone as the voice of the airline itself.

Among the most common calls are the requests for information on such subjects as weather conditions, baggage allowance, check-in time, and arrival time of flights, etc. A reservations agent will have to handle many kinds of situations. He must really know almost all the procedures and be prepared for any kind of call.

Passengers may call in to confirm their ongoing or return reservations. Most airlines, especially on international routes, require their passengers to confirm their continuing or return reservations. That is, they must call the airline to check the reservation and indicate whether they will use it. This protects the airline against no-shows, and it protects the passenger against the loss of his seat.

In many cases, there is an automatic cancellation if there is no confirmation (or reconfirmation, as it is sometimes called) within 24 hours of flight time. International reconfirmation is 72 hours. In addition to checking the passenger's reservation, the agent should also obtain a telephone contact where the passenger can be reached so that the agent can inform the passenger if there is a change about his flight.

Read the above passage carefully and answer the questions.

1. What is a reservations agent's principal job?
2. What other information should a reservations agent give the passengers besides reservations?
3. Why does a reservations agent sometimes ask a passenger for his telephone number?
4. Why must a reservations agent know almost all the airline procedures?

★ Further Reading 2

The Ticket Agent

The ticket agent handles all the same kinds of problems as the reservations agent, but with two important differences. First, he meets the public face-to-face at the airline ticket counter. His contact with the passenger is much more personal than the disembodied voice of the agent on the telephone. Second, the ticket agent is responsible for receiving money and making out tickets.

Air fares have become very complicated in the last few years. It is no longer simply a question of a first class versus an economy-class fare over a certain route. Many airlines, for instance, have high season and low season fares. Fares are higher and service is more frequent during the summer than the winter, the low season when there are fewer tourists. And on some airlines, there are also special fares for families traveling together. There is also a round trip discount, which is designed to attract passengers to buy a round trip ticket.

Read the above passage carefully and answer the questions.

1. What are the two important differences between the ticket agent and the reservations agent?
2. What are the high and low seasons?
3. Why should there be a round trip ticket?

★ Further Reading 3

E-Ticket

What is an e-ticket?

The e-ticket is the electronic image of a common paper ticket. It's a recording of some electronic numbers. Currently, it's the most advanced passenger ticket format, providing great convenience via electronic ticket reservation, payment, and boarding procedure while reducing greatly the airline cost. It's a much better choice than the common passenger ticket.

What're the advantages to use e-tickets?

Before—Buy traditional paper tickets

When you needed to take a flight, you must call the airline ticket booth to ask for information about flights, to book the ticket, and pay in cash. It cost you money and time!

When you knew that you had to take the early flight the next day and the ticket booth was closed already, when your flight was about to take off in 90 minutes and the ticket was not purchased yet, when you wanted to change the day to fly somewhere else and you were scared by expensive long distance calls and the complex procedure, what to do?

Now—Buy e-tickets

Once you have used the e-ticket service involving many major airlines provided by websites, you will own your own ticket service center. This is a completely different feeling. No more waiting before an easy boarding!

The e-ticket doesn't have to be delivered to you. When you have purchased one, you can get on board via valid certificate and your trip sheet ID. It will take no more than 10 minutes to apply through the phone or on the internet for a date modification. Special prices promoted by airlines especially for e-tickets will help you to save cost.

Unit 2

Check-in Service

🔹 *Look at the following check-in procedures. Can you put them in the right order?*

1. Filling up the information form of passengers' amount and baggage

2. Notifying the meal supplement

3. Notifying the chief steward of the passengers' amount and information about any important and special ones

4. Showing Flight Information Boards

5. Issuing boarding pass

6. Weighing each checked bag

7. Handing in tickets and the preparactive form of the departure flight to the conservator

8. Checking the amount of tickets and boarding passes

9. Checking airline tickets and valid ID cards

10. Assisting to look for the unboarded passenagers

11. Attaching a baggage sticker to each checked bag

12. Checking the amount and accepting the back-up passengers

13. Verifying the passengers' passport and visa if traveling internationally

14. Instructing each passenger to proceed to the appropriate concourse and gate for flight departure

Unit 2 Check-in Service

➕ *Now answer the questions.*

1. What are valid travel documents?
2. What's the limitation for the check-in baggage?
3. What are the provisions for liquid items in carry-on baggage?

➕ *Suppose you are a clerk at the check-in counter of Beijing Capital International Airport and giving passengers some information about check- in. Here are some useful sentences.*

> For domestic flights, ...arrive at the airport...before the scheduled flight of departure and check-in.
> For international flights, ...arrive at the airport ...before the scheduled flight of departure and check-in.
> ...with the ticket and personal effective statements.
> The airline will stop check-in ... before the scheduled departure time.
> Checking in online saves you time at the airport, and enables you to print your boarding passes from the comfort of your home or office.
> The luggage allowance and requirements at Beijing Capital International Airport are...

➕ *What is a boarding pass? And what information can you get from the following boarding pass?*

Dialogue—Passenger Check-in (1) 办理登机手续

Setting: It's time for passengers who are going to take Flight SQ821 to check in.

P1: Hello. I'd like to check in for flight number SQ821 to Singapore.

C: May I see your passport and ticket please?

P1: Yes, here you are.

C: Very good. Would you prefer aisle or window seat?

P1: Window seat please.

C: OK. Here are your ticket and passport, and here is your boarding pass.

P1: Thank you.

C: You're welcome.

C: Good morining.

P2: Good morning. Can I check in here for SQ821?

C: Yes, may I have your ticket and passport, please?

P2: Here you are.

C: Do you have any baggage to check in?

P2: Yes, I have one.

C: Please put it on the conveyor belt.

P2: OK. Could I take this briefcase as my hand baggage?

C: That's all right. What kind of seat do you prefer?

P2: Please give me a window seat.

C: I'm sorry. No more window seats are avaiable. Will the aisle seat be all right?

P2: That's okay.

C: Here are your ticket and passport, and here are your boarding pass and baggage check.

VOCABULARY ASSISTANT

aisle seat 靠过道的座位   window seat 靠窗口的座位
conveyor belt 传送带   baggage check 行李牌

Complete the following dialogue and practice with your partner.

C: Good morning. 1_____, please? (请出示您的机票和身份证。)

P: Here you are.

C: 2_____. (请将您的行李放到秤上。)

P: Is that inside the free allowance?

C: Yes.

P: By the way, can I take this laptop as my hand baggage?

C: That's all right. 3_____? (请问您需要什么样的座位？)

Unit 2 Check-in Service

P: Window seat.
C: I'm sorry. 4_____. (靠窗的座位已经满了。) Will the aisle seat be all right?
P: It's OK.
C: Your ticket and ID Card, and 5_____. (这是您的登机牌和行李牌。)

Make up your own dialogues between flight attendants and passengers using the following sentence patterns.

Clerk at the check-in counter	**Passengers**
1. What can I do for you?	1. Can I check in at this counter?
2. Show me your ticket and passport please.	2. Here you are.
3. Have you got any baggage to check?	3. I prefer a window seat.
4. What kind of seat do you prefer?	4. Thank you very much.
5. Here are your boarding card and baggage checks.	

Make up your own dialogues with your partner according to the following condition.

At the check-in counter, Tom shows his ticket and passport. He has two pieces of baggage to check in. He wants a window seat. As all the window seats have been taken, he can only have an aisle seat.

Seat Preference

According to the model, make conversations with your partner by using the prompts given below.

Model 1:

C: Do you have any seat preference?
P: May I have a window seat in a non-smoking area?
C: I'm sorry all the window seats have been taken. Would an aisle seat be all right?
P: That's fine.

1. P: a window seat in a non-smoking area
   C: no window seat available

2. P: a heavy smoker/prefer a window seat in a smoking area
   C: smoking is not allowed

3. P: prefer a seat in the forward cabin away from the engine

C: that particular seat is not available/assign an aisle seat in the rear of the cabin
4. P: traveling with a baby/prefer a seat with more space for legs
   C: no such a particular seat on board/assign a seat by the aisle in the forward part of the cabin

Model 2:

> P: Good morning, miss. We're traveling together. Will you assign us two seats together in a non-smoking section?
> C: I'm afraid we don't have two vacant seats together in the non-smoking section. Would you prefer two aisle seats, with the aisle in between, or two window seats one behind the other?
> P: I guess the aisle seats would be OK.

1. P: request three seats together in the non-smoking section in the forward part of the cabin/window seat are better
   C: no such seats in the forward part of the cabin/reserve two seats together in the rear of the cabin
2. P: request two seats together by the window
   C: two seats together are not available/suggest two window seats with the one behind the other or two aisle seats with the aisle in between
3. P: four of us traveling together/request party seats away from the engine
   C: two are together/two are separated but close to each other

✈ Dialogue—Passenger Check-in (2) 办理登机手续

C: Thank you for waiting, sir.
P: Here are my passport and ticket.
C: Thank you. Are you travelling by yourself today, Mr. Green?
...
C: Mr. Green, I see that you are travelling to Hong Kong today. Is that your final destination?
P: Yes.
C: How many bags would you like to check in?
P: Two.
C: Sir, may I ask you a few questions about your baggage? Do you know all the contents of these bags?
P: Yes, everything inside belongs to me and I packed my own bags.
C: I see. Would you kindly place your bags on the conveyor belt?

...

P: Mr. Green, I see that you have no identification attached to your baggage. Would you like to write your name, city and phone number on these bags, so that you can easily identify them at your destination? Here are name labels for you.

C: Thank you. I'll fill them up right away.

...

P: Here you are.

C: Thank you. Mr. Green. I've checked two pieces of baggage on the Air China flight 981 to Hong Kong for you. Is that correct?

VOCABULARY ASSISTANT

destination 目的地　　content 物品
label 标签　　claim tag 认领牌
ticket jacket folder 机票夹

P: Yes.

C: I'll attach your claim tags to your ticket jacket folder. Mr. Green, would you prefer a smoking seat or a non-smoking seat?

P: A non-smoking window seat.

C: Mr. Green, your seat number is Row 14, A, a window seat in economy class in non-smoking section. Is that okay?

P: That's okay.

C: Here is your ticket and passport and this is your boarding pass. May I suggest that you keep these documents available as there may be security checks during the boarding process?

P: Thank you.

C: Thank you for choosing Air China and have a pleasant flight to Hong Kong.

Read the dialogue above carefully and answer these questions.

1. When checking in passengers, what would you say if they have waited for longer than 5 minutes?
2. How would you address the passenger by his/her name?
3. What questions would you usually ask the passengers about their baggage?
4. After check-in should you place all the documents directly into the passenger's hands or place them on the counter?

Read the following boarding information.

1. Mr. Li will check in two suitcases and two handbags. His seat number is 16A in economy class; boarding time: 10:15 a.m.; boarding gate: 20.
2. Miss Wang will check in one trunk and one large suitcase. Her seat number is 9K in non-smoking section; boarding time: 4:00 p.m.; boarding gate: 15.
3. Mr. Jackson will check in one suitcase, one wooden box and one bicycle. His seat number is 23D in non-smoking section; boarding time: 2:45 p.m.; boarding gate: 12.

Fill in the blanks with the given words.

| the conveyor belt | overweight | the limit | late | baggage |
| tickets and passports | check in | | | |

C: Good evening, sir.
P: Evening. Is this where we 1_____ for the flight to Hong Kong?
C: That's right, sir, Flight CA520.
P: I hope we're not 2_____.
C: No, there are still quite a lot of passengers to come. What's your name, please?
P: Peter Jackson, Mr. and Mrs. Jackson.
C: Mr. and Mrs. Jackson... May I see your 3_____, please?
P: Here you are.
C: Fine. Is this all your 4_____?
P: That's right. These two cases and the two smaller bags.
C: Would you lift them onto 5_____?
P: I hope they're not 6_____.
C: No. You're well within 7_____.

Discuss in a small group and say something about the official documents that a passenger needs during the trip.

Definitions	Name of the documents
★ A travel document which proves the identity	★
★ An official entry in a passport	★
★ An official paper which proves the vaccination against some diseases	★
★ An official paper to show the passenger having the right to board the flight	★

What sort of passport is it? And what information can you get from this passport?

Unit 2 Check-in Service

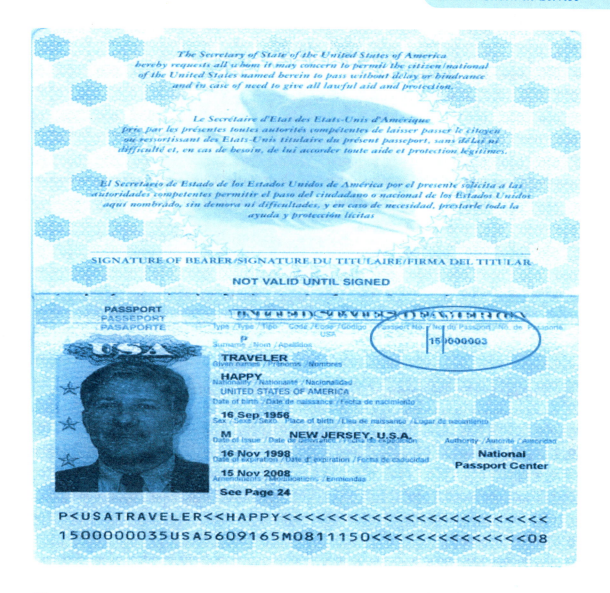

📋 **Dialogue—Inquiring about Check-in Information** 询问有关办理登机手续的信息

Setting: There are some passengers coming to the clerk to inquire about check-in place, time and procedures.

C: Good morning. What can I do for you?

P1: Is it the counter of China Southern Airlines?

C: That's right.

P1: Can I check in for flight CZ317?

C: No. It's too early.

P1: When will it start?

C: For international flights, we begin to check in one and a half hours before the departure time.

P1: I see. And when is the check-in counter closed?

C: Normally it is closed half an hour before the departure time.

P1: Thank you for your help.

C: You're welcome. See you later.

P1: See you later.

P2: Shall I check in at this counter?

C: Would you please show me your ticket? ... I'm sorry. You're not at the right counter. This is the counter of China Southern Airlines, you have to go to the counter of Hainan Airlines.

P2: Where is it then?

C: It is just over there.

P2: Thank you very much.

VOCABULARY ASSISTANT

China Southern Airlines 中国南方航空公司
departure time 起飞时间
normally 通常地

◆ Complete the following dialogue and practice with your partner.

P: It is the counter of Air China, isn't it?

C: Yes. 1_____? (有什么为您效劳的吗？)

P: I'm going to check in for flight CA925. 2_____? (我现在能办理登机手续吗？)

C: Yes, just right now. 3_____ (飞机将于九点半起飞), that is to say, it will depart from the Capital Airport in 35 minutes.

P: Oh. Am I too late?

C: No, not too late. But you should go to Gate 2 quickly after check-in. Most of the passengers have already boarded the plane. 4_____.(请出示您的机票和护照。)

P: Here you are.

C: OK. 5_____? (有要托运的行李吗？)

P: Yes, a suitcase.

C: OK. 6_____.(这是您的机票、护照、登机牌和行李牌。) A happy journey to you!

P: Thanks a lot. See you again!

◆ Do you know some other ways of checking in besides counter check-in?

Unit 2 Check-in Service

🔹 **Listen to the following passage carefully and complete the form about check-in options.**

_____ check-in

Using the Web check-in is to avoid the queues at the airport. It is quite easy and convienient. In just two steps you are ready to go: _____ and _____. Online check-in is possible between ____ ____ and _____ before the departure of the flight.

_____ check-in

At the airports, check-in machines offer passengers a way to save time. That's an easy way to handle your check-in on your own. First, insert your _____ into the machine. And then follow the instructions on the display and _____ -aisle or window. Within a few seconds, the self check-in kiosk will _____ your boarding pass.

🔹 **Read the above information carefully and show your partner how to use the check-in machine.**

Step 1: to insert _____
Step 2: to select _____
Step 3: to print _____
Step 4: to deliver _____

🔹 **Online Check-in and Kiosk Check-in**

Setting: You are an airport clerk and try to introduce the convinience of online check-in and kiosk check-in to passengers with the given information.

27

Checking in Through Internet

🍁 Check in for your flight from the convenience of your own computer.

🍁 Choose your seat and see where it's located on the aircraft.

🍁 Check in for your onward or return flight if it's within 24 hours.

🍁 Print your own boarding pass before you've even packed your suitcase.

Checking in at an Airport Kiosk

🍁 Easy to use, touch-screen kiosks enable you to check in within minutes.

🍁 Choose your seat and see where it's located on the aircraft.

🍁 Check in for your onward or return flight if it's within 24 hours.

🍁 Print your own boarding pass.

🍁 Available in English, French, German, Italian and Spanish.

Dialogue—Animals Check-in 宠物托运

P: I'm just wondering if I can take my dog with me.

C: Yes, but pets can only travel in cargo compartments according to our company regulations. You may not keep it in the cabin.

P: That's OK.

C: We charge your dog and its container as excess baggage.

P: Go ahead. Do you have pet containers for sale?

C: Yes, $5 each. Do you have the papers for your dog?

C: Yes, I have my dog's health card for quarantine inspection.

VOCABULARY ASSISTANT

pet 宠物　　cargo compartment 货仓　　charge 收费
container 箱、匣等容器　　excess baggage 超重行李
quarantine inspection 检疫检查

Make up your own dialogues with your partner according to the following condition.

John wants to take his small dog with him on a trip from Beijing to New York. He wants to keep it with him, but the airline doesn't permit pets in the passenger compartment and unfortunately, his dog will not be able to travel on the same flight with him. He has to check in his dog and its container as unaccompanied baggage.

> **Information Bank**
>
> ### *Checking in Animals and Items*
>
> Animals/Pets can be booked on some direct flights. It is the passengers' responsibility to ensure that they adhere to the regulations of the country to which they're traveling. All animals usually are transported in the cargo hold. Animals must be at least 10 weeks old. The cage in which the animal will travel is usually made of fiberglass. The animal must be able to fit comfortably. The cost of transport is usually advised by cargo. Airlines must be told a few weeks in advance that an animal will travel on a flight.
>
> Big items such as bicycles departing the airport must be boxed or bagged. Small instruments may qualify as hand baggage. Medium-sized instruments may be carried in the cabin if the passenger purchases an individual seat for the instruments.

★ Further Reading 1

Online Check-in Service 网上值机

Online check-in is a service that gives a possibility to check-in online to all passengers who have a ticket reservation before arriving at the airport. Passengers can enjoy check-in and select the seat from 24 hours up to 90 minutes prior to the departure time through Online Check-in web page of each Airline Company. It can be reached via internet. Simply entering your name, surname and flight details you'll be able to check-in online. To get more detail about online check-in, "Check In Help" link can be used.

Online check-in is available for the passengers with or without baggage. It is not need to register your baggage details while check-in. Baggage check-in process might be completed at the airport "baggage drop off point" or "online check-in desk." Desks are closed 45 minutes to international, 30 minutes to domestic flights schedule departing time. In case of excess baggage, passengers have to consider the time will be spent for excess baggage payment process. The Airline Company is not responsible for probable passenger delays due to excess baggage process.

Passengers without baggage and have online printed boarding card may go directly to the gate through to security control or otherwise baggage should be registered at "baggage drop off point" or "online check-in desk."

If you have already seat assignment in your reservation record, Online Check-in process will be completed accordingly then seat change facility can be used if it is requested. By using online check-in link user could login on system and by using "seat change" button the process can be completed.

Please be aware however, that additional airport security screening measures may increase the time required to complete the check-in process at the airport.

Read the above passage carefully and answer the questions.

1. What is Online Check-in?
2. What is the earliest and latest time for check-in?
3. How to use Online Check-in?
4. What should I do if I have baggage to check?
5. What happens if I want to change my seat assignment after I check in?

★ Further Reading 2

Passport and Visa 护照和签证

The passport is an official document issued by a competent public authority to nationals or to alien residents of the issuing country. Other than allowing access to another country, the passport can be used as a means of identification. Another purpose of the passport is to provide evidence of legal entry into another country.

There are several types of passport: normal passports; aliens passports that are issued to individuals living in a country of which they are not citizens; diplomatic or consular passports that are issued to diplomatic, consular and other governments supplied to regugees; joint passports (family passport) that are issued to husband and wife with/without child/children, or holder of the passport and child/children under a certain age, or two or more children.

A visa is an entry in a passport or other travel document made by an official of a government to indicate that the bearer has been granted authority to enter or re-enter the country concerned. It usually specifies the authorized length of stay, the period of validity and the number of entries allowed during that period.

Normally we have following types of visa:

Visitor visa also referred to as entry permit, entry visa, business visa or travel pass. It provides right of entry to another country.

Transit visa provides right of entry into another country only for the purpose of making travel connections onward to a third country. Transit without visa: many countries have made agreements that allow other nationals to transit their country without the need to obtain a visa.

Re-entry permits: where necessary, these permits entitle travelers to return to their country of domicile.

Exit permits: they entitle travelers to leave a country. These permits may be necessary for citizens to leave their own country of domicile.

Schengen visa: created in 1995, the Schengen is an agreement between several member states of the European Union, and effectively creates a "borderless" region known as the Schengen Area. Schengen states comprise: Austria, Belgium, France, Germany, Greece, Italy, Luxemburg, Netherlands, Portugal and Spain. The Schengen Agreement removes immigration controls for travel within and between these countries.

Over to you

1. What's the definition of the passport and what's the function of a visa?
2. Translate the following phrases into Chinese

   Visitor visa   Transit visa   Re-entry permits   Exit permits   Schengen visa

Complete the dialogue and practice with your partner.

1. According to our company regulations pets can only travel in cargo compartments.
2. Put your dog in the pet container.
3. We charge your dog and its container as excess baggage.
4. Do you have a health card for your dog?

Unit 3
Baggage Check-in Service

✚ *Tick items are prohibited both in carry-on luggage and check-in baggage.*

☐ walking stick ☐ firework ☐ fruit knives ☐ paints ☐ three kilos perfume
☐ liquid medicine ☐ lighter ☐ pushchair ☐ dry ice ☐ a tin of coca
☐ video camera ☐ razors ☐ laptops ☐ weed killer ☐ baseball bats

✚ *Match words in each column.*

carry-on luggage   免费行李
check-in baggage or checked luggage   超体积行李
free baggage allowance   超重行李
liquid items   托运行李
unaccompanied baggage   手提行李
excess baggage rate   液体物品
free allowance for luggage   行李标签
label/tag   免费行李重量限额
interline baggage   超重行李费
overweight baggage   无人伴随行李
over-size baggage   转机行李

Unit 3 Baggage Check-in Service

Try to answer the following questions.

1. What are the regulations regarding the carriage of liquids?
2. Are medium-sized instruments allowed to be carried in the cabin?
3. If you have brought something forbidden on board to the airport, what should you do?

Do you know the following restrictive provisions for check-in baggage at Beijng International Airport?

Limitation for hand luggage:

Domestic flight:
Total weight should be no more than 1_____. The size of each luggage should be no more than 2_____.

International flight:
Total weight should be no more than 3_____ (Some Airlines have their own special limits). The size of each luggage should be no more than 4_____ (The sum of length, width and height should be no more than 5_____).

Please note: The above are general provisions and different Airlines may have their own standards. Please check your flight tickets for specific information.

Dialogue—Baggage Check-in 行李托运

Setting: It's the time for passengers who are going to take Flight SU574 to check in.

C: Good morning.
P: Good morning. Can I check in here for SU574 to Moscow?
C: Yes, may I have your ticket and passport, please?
P: Here you are.
C: Do you have any baggage to check in?
P: Yes, I have 2 pieces.
C: Please put your two pieces of baggage on the conveyor belt one by one.
P: OK. Could I take this briefcase as my hand baggage?
C: That's all right. What kind of seat do you prefer?
P: Please give me an aisle seat.
C: Here is your ticket and passport, and here is your boarding pass and baggage checks.
P: Thank you very much.
C: Have a nice trip.

🔹 **Do you know the names of these bags? Match each picture with a proper English name.**

shoulder bag   rolling luggage   hand bag   laptop bag   carry-on bag
briefcase   suitcase   travel pack   backpack   waist pack

🔹 **Work in pairs and complete the dialogue with your partner.**

C: 1_____.（下午好，请出示您的机票和护照。）

P: Here you are.

C: 2_____?（您有行李要托运吗？）

P: Yes, one box.

C: 3_____?（请放到称上好吗？）I'm going to weigh it.

> **VOCABULARY ASSISTANT**
> first class 头等舱　　　exceed 超出
> allowance 规定　　　　overweight 超重

P: Ok. By the way, could you tell me how many kilos of free baggage each passenger is allowed?

C: The baggage allowance is different according to the class of your ticket. What class are you traveling?

P: First class.

C: 4_____.（头等舱的旅客可以免费托运40公斤的行李。）

P: How many pieces of baggage can I carry onto the plane?

C: Passengers holding first tickets may carry 2 pieces within the total weight of 5 kg onto the plane.

P: If my baggage exceeds the allowance, what should I do?

C: 5_____.（如果行李的重量超出了规定的范围，我们就要对超出的份量收费了。）

P: I see. Thank you very much for your information.

C: 6_____.（不客气，这是您的登机牌和行李托运牌。）

P: Good-bye!

Unit 3 Baggage Check-in Service

Dialogue—Carry-on Baggage (1) 随身携带的行李

C: Miss Li, I'm afraid you have got too much hand-carry baggage. We have a limit of hand-carry baggage for every passenger. This is to ensure the maximum safety and comfort for all passengers.

P: I see.

C: I would like to suggest that you reduce the number of your items of hand-carry baggage and I'll take the rest as checked baggage.

P: Sure.

C: Miss Li, these are two tags for your hand-carry bags. Please place them on your hand-carry bags. It shows that you have checked in your hand-carry baggage.

P: I see. Thank you.

VOCABULARY ASSISTANT

hand-carry baggage 手提行李   limit 限制
maximum 最大限度的   reduce 减少
checked baggage 托运行李   tag 标签

---

a. Good. But I still think that you carry too much hand baggage with you.

b. Well, I may as well take it as checked baggage.

c. So I still suggest you reduce the number of your items of hand baggage and take the rest as checked baggage.

d. Mr. Liu, I'm afraid that you can't take that bag as hand bag.

e. I've traveled a lot, but my hand baggage has never been weighed before.

f. It seems too big and may be too heavy as well. Let me explain it to you. The size and weight of hand baggage are limited by our regulations. The maximum is 20 centimeters by 40 centimeters by 55 centimeters in volume and 5 kilos in weight.

g. That's OK.

h. We have a limit of hand baggage for each passenger. This is to ensure maximum safety and comfort for all of our passengers.

i. I can manage myself.

j. Why not?

k. Here the rules are strictly followed.

l. I see.

VOCABULARY ASSISTANT

regulation 规定　　maximum 最大量
centimeter 厘米　　volume 体积、容积
strictly 严格地　　ensure 确保

◆ Rearrange the dialogue in the correct order.

◆ Each airline company has its own policy on carry-on baggage. Suppose you work at the check-in counter of United Airlines, and explain the carry-on baggage allowance to passengers who travel worldwide by using the given information.

For travel worldwide
one bag and one personal item such as a purse, briefcase, or laptop computer.

Carry-on bag
fit under the seat or in the overhead bin

Carry-on bag dimensions
not be more than 9" x 14" x 22" (length + width + height) or 45 linear inches (the length, height and width added together)

◆ **Dialogue—Carry-on Baggage（2）随身携带的行李**

C: Would you please put your folding bicycle on the scale?

P: I'm told that it is a free carry-on item and should not be weighed.

C: Mr. Li, maybe you were misinformed. According to regulations, a bicycle is not a free carry-on item. An overcoat, an umbrella, some reasonable reading matter and so on are carried free of charge and they need not be weighed. They are free carry-on items.

P: Well then, I have a few kilos overweight.

VOCABULARY ASSISTANT

folding bicycle 折叠式自行车
inform 通知、告知　　reasonable 适当的

Unit 3 Baggage Check-in Service

🔹 Translate the following regulation of carry-on baggage into Chinese.

According to regulations, a bicycle is not a free carry-on item. An overcoat, an umbrella, some reasonable reading matter and so on are carried free of charge and they need not be weighed. They are free carry-on items.

🔹 Listen to the statement and complete the following information on baggage.

Baggage refers to personal property that passengers take on their travels. According to the transportation authorities, baggage carried by Air China can be classified as _____ and _____.

Unchecked baggage should be suitable for placing into the closed overhead compartment or under the seat in front of passengers.

A. First and business class passengers are allowed ____ _____ carry-on bag that cannot exceed _____ in weight.

B. Economy class passengers are allowed _____ carry-on bag that cannot exceed _____ in weight and dimensions of _____ in length, _____ in width and _____ in height.

C. Baggage exceeding the above free baggage allowance should be checked.

—Maximum weight of each baggage should not exceed _____, and the maximum dimension should not exceed _____. The baggage exceeding the above allowance should be transported as freight.

—Minimum weight of each baggage should not be less than _____, and the minimum dimension should not be less than _____.

If the bags exceed the weight limit specified, the excess baggage charge per kilogram is _____ of the highest normal direct adult one way (Y class) fare.

🔹 Try to answer the following questions

1. What's the excess baggage?
2. What's the over-size baggage?

🔹 Think it over

If a passenger has brought overweight baggage to the airport, what should he/she do?

✈ **Introduce the baggage limitation to your passengers with the help of given information.**

Unchecked baggage (free carry-on articles)

A. First and business class passengers are allowed two carry-on bags that cannot exceed 5 kg in weight.

B. Economy class passengers are allowed one carry-on bag that cannot exceed 5 kg (11 lbs) in weight and dimensions of 55 cm (21 inches) in length, 40 cm (15 inches) in width and 20 cm (7 inches) in height.

C. Baggage exceeding the above free baggage allowance should be checked.

Articles that can not be transported in carry-on baggage

Passengers are not allowed to carry in their carry-on baggage any dangerous articles such as guns, knives, sharp or lethal weapons, or animals.

Checked baggage

A. Travel box, travel bag and handbag should be locked to avoid theft.

B. More than two bags cannot be bundled into one.

C. Additional articles should not be inserted in the baggage.

D. Bamboo baskets, net bags, ropes, straw bags, plastic bags cannot be wrapped around the baggage.

E. Passengers' name, detailed address, and phone number should be written inside and outside the baggage.

Limitation of checked baggage weight and volume

—Maximum weight of each baggage should not exceed 45 kg, and the maximum dimension should not exceed $100 \times 60 \times 40$ cm³. The baggage exceeding the above allowance should be transported as freight.

—Minimum weight of each baggage should not be less than 2 kg, and the minimum dimension should not be less than $30 \times 10 \times 20$ cm³. The baggage that exceeding the above allowance cannot be transported as checked baggage alone.

✈ **Dialogue—Overweight Baggage (1) 行李超重**

C: Good afternoon, miss. Your ticket and passport please.

P: Here you are.

C: Thank you. Do you have any baggage to check in?

P: Yes, two pieces.

C: Would you put them on the scale? I'll weigh them.

P: OK.

C: Your baggage is 16 kilos. The total weight of baggage for passengers holding economic-class tickets is 10 kilos. Yours is 6 kilos overweight.

Unit 3 Baggage Check-in Service

P: What should I do?
C: I'm afraid you have to pay a charge for it.
P: How much would that be?
C: You should pay ￥240.
P: OK. Here is the money.
C: OK. And here is your receipt, boarding pass and baggage check.
P: Good-bye!

The following sentences could go together to form a full dialogue, but they are in the wrong order. Put them right.

a. The weight allowance for a suitcase is 23kg, but this one is 28kg. I'm afraid you'll have to remove some items from your suitcase or pay for the extra weight.
b. All right then. Thank you very much.
c. Good afternoon.
d. OK. Could you please place the suitcase on the belt?
e. Just across there on the left, you see the big yellow sign?
f. Next, please.
g. Yes, I see it. May I leave my suitcase here?
h. Sorry, sir, this bag is over the weight allowance.
i. Good afternoon. Can I have your ticket and passport, please?
j. I will write a ticket for you and you will have to pay it at the extra weight desk.
k. My pleasure.
l. Sure.
m. Sorry, you can't. You have to take it with you. And here is your ticket and passport too. When you come back, I will check you in.
n. Thank you.
o. Huh?
p. OK, so how much do I have to pay?
q. And where is it?
r. Here you are.

Translate the following useful sentences into English.

1. 您要交运几件行李？
2. 请您把箱子放在磅秤上，我要称称重量。

3. 您的行李重20公斤。持经济舱客票的旅客可以携带两件总重量不超过10公斤的行李登机。您的行李超重10斤，恐怕您要付费了。
4. 免费行李根据所乘坐的舱位不同而不同。
5. 这是您的收据。给您机票、护照、登机牌和行李牌。

Dialogue—Overweight Baggage (2) 行李超重

C: Good morning. Your ticket and passport, please.

P: Here you are.

C: Do you have any baggage to check in?

P: Yes, I have got a box.

C: Please put it on the scale. I'll weigh it. I'm afraid your baggage is overweight.

P: What should I do?

C: I suggest you send it as unaccompanied baggage.

P: What is unaccompanied baggage?

C: It means the baggage is shipped as cargo. It does not travel on the same flight as you.

P: I see. How much is that?

C: The same as cargo. It's cheaper than overweight fee. That is 20 Yuan.

P: OK. Here is the money.

C: Here is your ticket, passport, baggage check and receipt for unaccompanied baggage.

Complete the following dialogue with proper sentences given below.

C: I'm afraid that your excess baggage will not be able to go with you, because 1_____.

P: Then, what shall we do with the baggage?

C: 2_____.

P: What do you mean by unaccompanied baggage.

C: It means 3_____.

P: I see. What's the rate for that?

C: The same as cargo. 4_____.

P: Okay, 5_____.

a. You pay much less than the excess baggage charge.
b. I suggest you send it as unaccompanied baggage.
c. Let it go as cargo.
d. we have a full load for the flight today.
e. The baggage is shipped as cargo.

Unit 3 Baggage Check-in Service

🔹 **John came to China a few days ago. Now he is going back to America. He brought many gifts for his family so his baggage is not within the weight allowance. Please give him some advice on how to deal with the excess baggage. Here are some useful sentence patterns.**

- I'm afraid you'll have to remove some items from your suitcase or pay for the extra weight.
- We have to treat your baggage as overweight baggage. I'm afraid you have to pay for it.
- I suggest you send this suitcase as unaccompanied baggage.
- The baggage is shipped as cargo. It does not travel on the same flight as you.
- The same as cargo. You pay much less than the excess baggage charge.

🔹 **Make up your own dialogues with your partner according to the given condition.**

Mary's baggage is overweight and her excess baggage will not be able to go with her, because of a full load for the flight. She has to send the excess baggage as unaccompanied baggage.

🔹 **Think it over.**

What would you suggest the passengers whose baggage is oversize to do?

🔹 **Listen to the dialogue and fill in the blanks with the missing information while listening.**

C: Hello, sir. Are you going to check in for flight XW105?

P: Yes. Here is my ticket.

C: Your ticket is OK. What baggage are you going to check?

P: I check these two cardboard boxes only.

C: Your small one is OK. But the other one is too big.

P: They only weigh 22 kg together, only 2 kg overweight.

C: I don't mean they are 1_____ too much. I mean that one is 2_____. Look, this is 120 cm long, 60 cm wide and 40 cm high. That one is 75 cm long, 40 cm wide and 30 cm high. The big one is over the 3_____.

P: What's the limitation?

C: The 4_____ for each economy-class passenger is two pieces, and the sum of the 5_____ of each must not exceed 158 cm, but the sum of the length, width and

41

height for the two pieces must not exceed 273 cm.

P: What should I do then?

C: The big box should be handled as 6_____. You should pay RMB 25.

P: OK, here is the money.

C: Here are your boarding pass, baggage checks and 7_____ for the overweight baggage.

P: Thank you very much.

Dialogue—Oversize Baggage 超体积行李

C: How do you do?

P: How do you do?

C: Your ticket and passport, please.

P: Here you are.

C: What baggage do you want to check in?

P: I have got two suitcases.

C: This big one is over the length limit.

P: What should I do?

C: Would you like to send it as unaccompanied baggage?

P: No, I want all the baggage to travel with me.

C: I see. We have to treat your baggage as overweight baggage. You have to pay for that.

P: Ok, how much will you charge me?

C: You have to pay 50 yuan as excess charge.

P: Here's the money.

C: Here are your boarding pass, baggage checks and receipt for the overweight baggage.

P: Thank you very much.

C: You're welcome.

Translate the following sentences into English.

1. 不在规定的免费行李范围内。
2. 每件行李的长宽高总和应不超过158厘米。
3. 这件行李超过了长度限制。
4. 您愿意把这个大箱子作为无人伴随行李托运吗？
5. 您应付人民币200元的超重费。

Complete the following dialogue and practice with your partner.

C: Good morning. Can I help you?

P: Good morning, Miss. Is this the counter for Flight CA351?

C: Yes. Can I have your ticket and passport?

P: Here you are.

C: Your ticket is OK. What baggage are you going to check in?

P: Only two boxes.

C: It seems that one box is too big. 1_____? (您量过您的行李吗？)

P: I haven't measured it. But I have weighed them. They are only 19kg together. It is within the free baggage allowance.

C: I don't mean they are overweight. I mean one of them is too long. How long is this box?

P: Sorry, I don't know.

C: Let me measure. 2_____. (这个箱子长92厘米，宽65厘米，高44厘米。) That one is 65 cm long, 40 cm wide and 25 cm high. The big one is over the length limit.

P: What's the limit?

C: The free baggage allowance for each economy-class passenger is two pieces, and 3_____,(每个行李长宽高总和不应超过158厘米，) and the sum of the two pieces must not exceed 273 cm.

P: What should I do them?

C: 4_____? (您愿意把这个大箱子作为无人伴随行李托运吗？)

P: No, I want all the baggage to travel with me.

C: I see. We have to treat your baggage as overweight baggage. 5_____. (您应付25元的超重费。)

P: Here is the money.

C: Here are your boarding pass, baggage checks and receipt for the overweight baggage.

P: Thank you very much.

 Make up your own dialogues with your partner according to the following conditions.

(1) A is going to take Flight XW342 to Munich. He has reserved a first class seat. At the check-in counter, the clerk finds that one piece of his baggage is over volume and he has to pay a charge for it.

(2) B brought a bicycle for her nephew, but the packing is over-size. The clerk at the check-in counter suggests her to send the bike as unaccompanied baggage to save her the excess baggage charge. She accepts her suggestion.

 **Discussion**

You notice that your passenger is carrying a set of delicate glassware. What kind of advice will you give him? Do you think that your airline will be responsible for the damage?

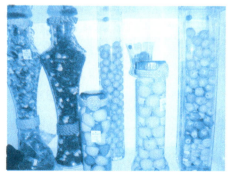

 **Dialogue—Fragile Baggage (1) 易碎行李**

C: Sir, may I know what's inside the case?

P: Some cloisonne. This is very delicate. You'd better handle with care.

C: Certainly, we will respect and take care of your bag properly and I'll place a fragile sticker on the bag.

P: What for?

C: Sir, I'm making your bag "fragile" to ensure the baggage handlers treat it with care.

P: Thank you.

VOCABULARY ASSISTANT

cloisonne 景泰蓝　delicate 易碎的　handle 对待;处理
sticker 标签　　　treat 对待;处理

Dialogue—Fragile Baggage (2) 易碎行李

P: Afternoon, miss. I want to check in this cardboard case to Sydney.

C: No problem. What's inside, may I ask?

P: A tea set. It's very delicate. Would you please remind your baggage handler to ship it carefully?

C: Certainly. But your case requires strict packing. I notice that you didn't seal your case properly. Please repack and make it sure that it's safe enough to be shipped.

P: OK. I'll redo it for the sake of safety.

P: Then I'll place a fragile sticker on the case to remind the baggage handlers to treat it with care.

P: Thank you for your consideration.

VOCABULARY ASSISTANT

cardboard case 纸箱子　　　remind 提醒
strict 严格的　　seal 密封　　redo 重做
for the sake of 出于……的原因

Dialogue—Baggage with Limited Liability 有限责任

C: Mr. Li, do you notice that the strap is broken?

P: Oh, no. I didn't notice that.

C: I'm afraid this box is considered improperly packed for carriage. We will handle it with care, but Air China cannot be responsible for damage or breakage.

P: I'm sorry but I have no time to repack.

C: Please complete a Limited Release Tag and we'll ship the box.

P: Okay

...

P: Here is the tag.

...

C: Would you sign here to verify that I've explained this to you?

P: Okay. Here you are.

C: Thank you.

> **VOCABULARY ASSISTANT**
>
> strap 带子   improperly 不适当地
> pack 包装   damage 损坏   breakage 破损
> Limited Release Tag 免除责任行李牌

Dialogue—Acceptance of Excess Baggage 超重行李

C: Mr. Wang, you have more than 5 pieces of excess baggage.

P: Yes, I'm going to emigrate to the United Kingdom.

C: I'm afraid the flight is very full today and we are unable to carry so much passenger baggage.

P: Well, all my baggage has to go with me because inside these boxes are our clothing and daily necessities. We need them right after we arrive in London.

C: Let me check with cargo section to see if they have space available.

...

(Space is available)

C: Mr. Wang, I'm happy to tell you we do have space for boxes. For your future flights with Air China, you can reserve space by calling our reservation office.

P: I will. Thank you.

...

(Space is not available)

C: Mr. Wang, I'm sorry to tell you that today's flight is full and we cannot accept all of your baggage. Would you be able to reduce your check-in baggage? If not, you can reschedule your trip for the coming Saturday's flight.

Dialogue—Pooled Baggage 合并计算行李

C: Mr. Liu, the allowance is 20 kilos for each passenger. Your baggage is 5 kilos overweight. Mr. Zhang's baggage weighs 12 kilos. He is well inside the limit. Are you from the same company traveling together for the entire journey?

P: Yea, Mr. Zhang and I are from Peking University and we are going together to the United States for an academic conference.

C: I see. I will pool your baggage and save you the excess baggage charge.

VOCABULARY ASSISTANT

academic conference 学术会议
pool 共有、共享、联营

Information Bank

Pooled Baggage

When two or more passengers traveling as one party to a common destination point or point of stopover via the same flight, present themselves and their baggage for traveling at the same time and place, they will be permitted a total free baggage allowance equal to the combination of their individual free baggage allowance. Baggage in excess of the combined maximum allowance will be subject to the excess baggage charge.

Read the above dialogue carefully and make up a similar one according to the given situation.

A and B are traveling together to San Francisco after the Olympic Games. A's baggage is 5 kilos overweight. The clerk at the check-in counter wants him to pay a charge. But he says his friend, B's baggage weighs 15 kilos and the clerk can pool their baggage and save them the excess baggage charge. The clerk accepts his suggestion.

Dialogue—Interlined Baggage 联运行李

(*At the check-in counter*)

P: My bags go to San Francisco first.

Unit 3 Baggage Check-in Service

C: Miss Chen, your destination is Houston, isn't it?

P: Yes, but I'll go to San Francisco first for a connection.

C: You can check-in your baggage all the way through to Houston.

P: Can I? I didn't know about that.

C: I'll have your baggage checked through and you don't have to claim and transfer it in San Francisco Airport.

P: It goes directly to Houston?

C: Yes, isn't it convenient?

P: Yes, it certainly is.

...

C: Your bags are OK. Half of the label goes on your bag and the other on your ticket. You match the two numbers and make sure it's yours.

VOCABULARY ASSISTANT

connection 转机　　claim 申报
convenient 方便

Complete the dialogue with the proper given words and practice with your partner.

C: Do you have any _____?

P: Yes. These two suitcases. I'll go to Shanghai first then take a connecting flight to Wolverhampton.

C: I see. You will _____ the flight in Shanghai but you don't have to _____ your baggage and _____ it there. Our airlines can _____ your baggage all the way through to _____. Actually, as soon as the flight arrives in Shanghai the baggage handlers will transfer it to the _____ that is bound for Wolverhampton. You just _____ a rest in the _____ and _____ your next flight.

P: You can ship my baggage directly to Wolverhampon?

C: Sure. But I will _____ your suitcase as the _____. The baggage handler will _____ them. It saves time and trouble, doesn't it?

P: It certainly does.

claim	ship	take	wait for	take care of
change	transfer	label	interlined baggage	
checked baggage		your destination		
connecting flight		transit lounge		

47

Information Bank

Interline Baggage

For your convenience, baggage can be checked in from your point of origin straight through to your final destination. Please allow a minimum of 75 minutes for connections for mainland travelers and 2 hours for international travelers. Passengers departing with a domestic connection must have baggage checked.

Read the above dialogue carefully and make up a similar one according to the given situation.

Wang Jun is traveling from Qingdao to New Zealand with a connecting flight at Singapore. When he starts to check in his baggage as far as Singapore, the clerk at the check-in counter informs him that he can check in his baggage all the way through to New Zealand.

Baggage tips

Here are some handy tips you may introduce to your customers to follow.

Checked baggage

Label your bags inside and out with your name, destination address, email address and mobile or cell number.	Fragile items should be packed in a container capable of withstanding airport and baggage processes.
Make sure you know your free allowance for baggage which goes in the aircraft hold.	Make sure there are no loose straps or other items hanging from the bag, this applies particularly for rucksacks.
Remember that you won't have access to your checked baggage on board the flight.	Boxes or crates should be within the dimensions (H+W+L): 158 cm (62 in) and be packed in a sturdy manner.

Unit 3 Baggage Check-in Service

| Any items over your allowance will be charged as excess baggage. | Don't pack any valuables in your checked baggage. |

Hand baggage

Make sure you know your hand baggage allowance.

Do not take sharp objects in your hand baggage that will be confiscated at security.

Cigarette lighters are not permitted in hand baggage.

Make sure you take medication, important documents, valuable items and cash in your hand baggage.

Any items over your allowance will be charged as excess baggage.

Read the following useful expressions and translate them into Chinese.

1. the size and weight of hand baggage are limited by our regulations
2. to ensure maximum safety and comfort for all the passengers
3. to make sure there are no loose straps or other items hanging from the bag
4. to check in the baggage all the way through to the destination

Language Practice.

Setting: You are working at the check-in counter. Try to solve the following check-in problems by making dialogues with your partner.

Mr. Scott, a heavy smoker, checks in Flight CA671 from Beijing to Ottawa

Travel documents:
Passport
Ticket: Economy class
Seat preference:
Passenger requests a window seat
No window seat available/no smoking on board
Agent suggests an aisle seat
Baggage:
2 pieces of baggage (4 kilos over)
4 pieces of carry-on baggage
Agent persuades him to reduce some of them
Boarding time: 13:45
Boarding gate: 13

Mr. Zhao and his daughter want to take MU 312 leaving Hangzhou for Washington D.C.

Travel document:
Passport
Tickets: China Airline tickets: first class
Seat preference:
Request: 2 seats together
No party seats
Agent suggests 2 aisle seats or 2 window seats
Baggage:
3 pieces of baggage (5 kilos over)
3 pieces of carry-on baggage
Boarding time: 6:40
Boarding gate: 6

Unit 4

Security Check

■ *Look at these items below. Point out which ones are prohibited items in cabin baggage only and which ones are even prohibited in checked-in luggage generally?*

🛫 **Read the statements below and discuss with your partner about the security check procedures.**

"Ladies and gentlemen! Please form a line and have your ID cards and passports, plane tickets and boarding cards ready for inspection. Thank you for your cooperation."

"Ladies and gentlemen, please stand behind the yellow line with your papers."

"Ladies and gentlemen! We will start the security checking now. It would help us if you could take out your bags anything like cigarettes, keys, lighters, and calculators. Thank you for your cooperation."

"Please put your carry-on baggage on this belt and go through this door. Thank you for your cooperation."

🛫 **Dialogue—Managing the Crowds（1）疏导人群**

P: Excuse me. Could you please tell me which line is for Hong Kong? I'm flying on CA925.
C: Anyone is OK. But there are fewer passengers in Line One.
P: Oh, thanks.

🛫 **Dialogue—Managing the Crowds（2）疏导人群**

P: Listen! It's time for us to board the flight. Let's hurry up.
C: Don't be in such a hurry. Are you going to take flight CZ369?

P: Yes, we are.

C: This way please. You have to go through the security check first.

P: Oh, I see. Thanks.

Dialogue—Checking the Pass (1) 通行检查

C: Good morning, sir. Please show me your ticket, boarding card and passport.

P: Here you are.

C: What is your destination?

P: I'm going to Hong Kong.

C: OK. You can pass the gate with your luggage, please.

P: Thanks a lot. Bye.

C: Bye. Wish you a pleasant journey.

Dialogue—Checking the Pass (2) 通行检查

C: Please show me your ticket, boarding card and passport.

P: Boarding card?

C: Oh, you haven't got a boarding card yet? Sorry, you need to check in first.

P: Where can I do that?

C: Over there. Do you see that indicator board? Just under that.

P: Oh, thanks.

C: You are welcome. Please go there with your luggage, check in and get a boarding card.

At the Front of the Belt 行李传送带旁

Read the statements below and get familiar with the formalities of security check.

- "Ladies and gentlemen, please form a line and go through the gate one by one."
- "Excuse me, but you are not allowed to pass through the gate at the same time. Please do it one by one."
- "Please take off your shoes and put them in this basket before going through the gate, thanks."
- "Please put your lighter, cigarettes, mobile, calculators and keys on the tray."

- "Don't worry! The mat has been disinfected."
- "Please go through that detection gate, and the staff may give you a personal search."
- "Please put your carry-on baggage on that belt, which will take it into the electronic metal detector to have a check."

- "Security check is for the safety of the aircraft and all passengers. This is a common practice all over the world. All airlines, both domestic and international, require security check, including personal search."
- "Please just put your check baggage, and your carry-on baggage will be checked later."

Make up dialogues according to the following situations given.

(1) Mr. Illman who is going to New York didn't check in and get a boarding card.

(2) Mrs. Wright is worried about the mat; she won't take off her shoes because she thinks the mat is very dirty.

Translate the following sentences into Chinese.

(1) Beijing Capital Airport Security Check Station welcomes any comments or suggestions on any aspect of our service.

(2) Passengers refusing security screening are not allowed to board the aircraft or enter the airport terminal sterile area, and they will be responsible for any loss.

(3) For information about passengers' checked luggage, please refer to the airline's ground service department.

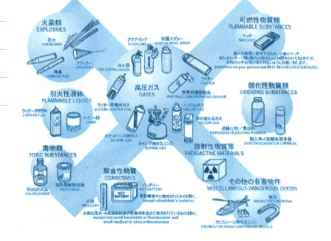

Unit 4 Security Check

Information Bank

All checked-in baggage will be inspected when you check in at the airline counter.

Before your baggage is checked in it will be inspected using x-ray equipment.

Your bags may also be opened as part of this inspection.

You may not re-open your bags once they have undergone inspection.

You may not carry knives or similar items on board. If you wish to take such items with you, you must put them in your check-in baggage before inspection. You must not carry knives or similar objects yourself.

Dialogue—Checking with Hand Detector 用手提检测仪检查

Listen to the dialogues and answer the questions.

VOCABULARY ASSISTANT	
buzz 嗡嗡作声	platform 平台
turn around 转过身	lighter 打火机
potter's knife 陶瓷刀	
within one month 在一个月之内	

What happened in the dialogues? How did the agent solve the problem? What have you learnt from these dialogues?

Translate the following sentences into Chinese.

Please switch on your digital camera. Thank you very much.

_____
_____

Sir, please open the bottle of mineral water and drink it, would you?

_____
_____

The work of security screening adheres to the principle of safety first, strict screening, civilized performance and courteous service.

_____
_____
_____

Dialogue—Checking Carry-on Luggage（1）检查随身携带行李

Listen to the dialogue with your partner and finish the exercises below.

Setting: Mr. Brown is going through the security check and he is required to put his bag on the belt and metal articles in the tray.

VOCABULARY ASSISTANT

unexposed 未曝光的　　film 胶卷
conveyor belt 传送带
loaded（相机）装好胶卷的
a shaving kit 一套剃须工具
souvenir 纪念品　　bother 打扰、麻烦

Dialogue—Checking Carry-on Luggage（2）检查随身携带行李

Setting: Miss Allison is going through the gate of security check. As the bell buzzes, the clerk has to stop her.

Unit 4 Security Check

VOCABULARY ASSISTANT

empty 清空,倒空
coin 硬币
X-ray X 射线

Dialogue—Checking Carry-on Luggage (3) 检查随身携带行李

Setting: Mr. Wright has something not allowed to be taken aboard. He is asked to leave it behind.

Dialogue—Checking Carry-on Luggage (4) 检查随身携带行李

Setting: Mr. Smith has bought a toy pistol for his son. Now he is going through the security check.

VOCABULARY ASSISTANT

toy 玩具   pistol 手枪   check 托运

Answer the question.

Do you know what articles should be prohibited on board from above dialogues?

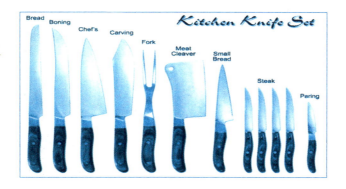

Information Bank

Security Check

All carry-on baggage is subject to inspection. Your carry-on baggage will be put through an x-ray machine and you yourself will have to walk through a metal detector. Your shoes may also be inspected if the metal detector registers something when you pass through. You may also be asked to open your bags and may be subject to a body search. Bringing any knives or similar items on board aircraft is strictly prohibited.

If any knives or other dangerous items are discovered in your possession, you will be asked to dispose of them.

Please translate the following items into Chinese.

1. The purpose of the security check is for the safety of the aircraft and all passengers.
2. This kind of thing is prohibited from being carried by passengers in accordance with the new regulations.

Make up dialogues according to the following situations given.

1. Mr. Victor wants to take his suitcase on board the aircraft, but there are some Chinese ancient craftwork knives in his suitcase.
2. Mrs. Thomas has a delicate bottle of Chinese perfume in her purse when she is going through the security check.

Dialogue—Patrolling in the Airport Terminal Sterile Area 在机场候机隔离区巡逻

Listen to the dialogues and fill out the blanks.

C: Whose briefcase is this?
P: It's mine.
C: 1_____?
P: Oh, it's also mine.
C: OK. 2_____?
P: Yes. I'm waiting for my daughter. 3_____.

C: I see. 4_____? It's very crowded here.
P: Sorry, I'll go there.

VOCABULARY ASSISTANT

the airport terminal sterile area 机场候机隔离区
briefcase 公文包

Read the dialogues with your partner and answer the questions below.

Dialogue—Special Circumstances (1) 特殊情境

C: Excuse me, sir. This way, please. Please show me your ticket, boarding card and passport.
P: I'm a diplomat. According to the international practice, our documents and luggage are exempt from examinations.
C: Sorry. That's true for the customs check but this is the security check which every passenger, including diplomats, must go through. This is also international practice.
P: I'm a counselor of Embassy in Shanghai. I enjoy diplomatic immunity.
C: I'm sorry. Even an ambassador has to go through this check. We implement this check for the safety of all the passengers including you. We hope you will cooperate with us.
P: What if I refuse the check?
C: If so, you will not be allowed to go on board. That is according to the Civil Aviation Regulations of our government.
P: All right. I give in this time. But I still want to write a letter to your government about this.
C: Sorry, I'm just an inspector. It is my responsibility to do things according to our government regulations. You could accuse me of doing something wrong, but in my opinion, as a diplomat, you should know how to respect the regulations of other countries.

VOCABULARY ASSISTANT

diplomat 外交人员   exempt 被免除的
counselor 参赞   diplomatic immunity 外交赦免权
implement 贯彻, 执行   refuse 拒绝   accuse 控告

Dialogue—Special Circumstances (2) 特殊情境

C: Whose box is it?
P: It's mine. Is it fine? May I take it away now?

C: Hold on a second, please. Maybe your porcelain is broken.

P: Really? Oh, no. Broken? Yes, I dropped it on the floor when I was coming to the airport in a hurry. I didn't think it was broken. You know, it is for my parents. What shall I do?

C: It's really a great pity. I feel sorry. However, there is no use crying over the spilt milk. I guess you might get another one in the duty-free shop.

P: May I go back there now?

C: Sure, you can. But may I know when your flight will take off?

P: At 14:50.

C: You still have 50 minutes.

P: Can I leave my other baggage here?

C: Oh, it is better if you take them with you. As you see, there are many people and things here.

P: OK. Thank you for your kind suggestions, anyway.

Answer the questions.

What happened in this dialogue? How did the clerk solve those problems? What have you learnt from this dialogue?

Packing Tips

Hand Luggage—What Not To Pack

You should always check the exact hand luggage allowance with your airline prior to packing. Most airlines have a hand baggage measurement gauge at check-in.

Take only one piece of hand luggage and make sure that your hand luggage does not contain:

Scissors	Razor blades
Knives with blades of any length	Household cutlery
Tweezers	Hypodermic needles (unless required for medical reasons)
Tool Toys/Replica guns (metal or plastic)	Catapults
Knitting needles	Sporting bats
Corkscrews	Walking/Hiking poles
Billiard, snooker or pool cues	Darts

If items are confiscated at security control you will not be compensated and, with the exception of unusual circumstances, the confiscated items will not be returned.

All Luggage—What Not To Pack

In addition to the restrictions on what is allowed in hand luggage, there are a number of items that must not be taken on board an aircraft, either as hand luggage or in the hold. Please do not pack the following anywhere in your carry-on or check-in luggage:

Flammable liquids and solids	Oxidisers
organic peroxides	gas cylinders
infectious substances	wet car cell batteries
instruments containing magnets	instruments containing mercury
magnetrons	fireworks
non-safety matches, fire lighters, lighter fuel	paints, thinners
poisons, arsenic, cyanide, weedkiller	acids, corrosives, alkalis, caustic soda
creosote, quicklime, oiled paper	radioactive materials

VOCABULARY ASSISTANT

scissor 剪刀　　cutlery 餐具　　tweezer 镊子　　hypodermic needles 皮下注射器针头
replica 复制品　　catapults 弹弓　　corkscrew 螺丝锥　　hike 远足
billiard 台球的　　snooker 桌球　　pool 撞球　　cue 球杆
dart 标枪,飞镖　　flammable 易燃的　　oxidiser 氧化物　　peroxide 过氧化物
gas cylinder 毒气筒　　infectious 有传染性的　　wet cell 湿电池
car battery 车用蓄电池　　magnet 磁铁　　mercury 汞　　magnetron 磁电管
thinner 稀释剂　　arsenic 砷　　cyanide 氰化物　　weedkiller 除草剂
corrosive 腐蚀剂　　alkali 碱金属　　caustic soda 苛性钠　　creosote 碳酸
quicklime 生石灰　　oiled paper 油纸　　radioactive 放射性的

◆ Dialogue—Setting Disputes 解决争执

Read the dialogue with your partner and make up dialogues according to the situations given below.

P: Hey, who is in charge of here?

C: How may I help you, sir?

P: Your man checked my bag for such a long time that I missed my flight. Tell me what I shall do.

C: Sir, please calm down and tell me what exactly happened. When did you come to the Security Check?

P: About 11:20.

C: Please show me your ticket. Oh, the departure time of your flight was 11:30, but you came to be checked at 11:20. There wasn't enough time for you to board the plane.

P: I still had 10 minutes left at that time. It was only because you spent too much time checking my bag that I missed my flight, so you should pay for my loss.

C: There is something unusual in your bag. In order to ensure the safety of all the passengers including you, and ensure the aircraft is safe, we must open your bag and have a special check.

P: Then what should I do now?

C: It is better for you to go to the No. 2 Check-in Counter to change your flight.

P: Fine. I'll go there.

Make up dialogues according to the situations given.

1. Mr. Muller travels with a competition fencing sword.
2. Mr. Carter brings 4 bottles of alcohol with him.

Dialogue—Supervising and Guarding the Aircraft (1) 监护航空器

Read the dialogue with your partner and finish the exercise.

C: Good morning, sir. May I have a look at your pass?

P: Here you are.

C: You are a maintenance mechanic?

P: Yes, I am a mechanic for United Airlines.

C: Fine. You may go, please.

Dialogue—Supervising and Guarding the Aircraft (2) 监护航空器

C: Good afternoon, sir. Show me your pass, please?

P: Oh, sorry. I forgot it.

C: As you know, it is a rule that all staff members at this airport should carry passes with them.

P: But I've an urgent appointment. Oh, I have my airlines' ID card with me.

C: Well, wait for a second. I'll report it to my superior. Tell me your name and job, please.

P: Newt Illman, I'm a pilot.

...

C: OK, you may go. Next time don't forget to bring your pass with you.

Dialogue—Supervising and Guarding the Aircraft (3) 监护航空器

C: Good morning, sir. What are you going to do on board?

P: I'm the maintenance mechanic of this plane.

C: Show me your pass, please.

P: Here you are.

C: Sorry, sir. But I have to make you wait here.

P: Why? I've something very important to do on board.
C: Well, I'm sorry. You must wait. Look, passengers are still getting off the plane and it's really crowded now. You may go on board after they all leave.
P: How long will it take?
C: A few minutes.

VOCABULARY ASSISTANT

pilot 飞行员   maintenance mechanic 机械师
United Airlines 美联航

Answer the questions.

How to supervise and guard the aircraft at the airport?

★ Further Reading 1

The Importance of Security Check

As a result of the airplane hijackings that have taken place with increasing frequency, almost all airports all over the world have instituted pre-boarding security checks for weapons and even, in some places, for potentially dangerous or demented persons. These procedures usually consist of a baggage search and some sort of personal search for concealed weapons. And this is ordinarily done with an electronic metal detector.

In almost all cases, the actual search is carried out by government agents rather than airline personnel. A few passengers will complain about it in no uncertain terms. The point that the agent must make, of course, is that the search is being made for the passenger's own protection. Most passengers will readily accept this fact and endure the brief unpleasantness with good humor. And the fact is, the security regulations have really worked. Hijackings have been cut to zero or near zero in those countries with the strictest regulations.

VOCABULARY ASSISTANT

hijacking 劫机   frequency 频率
demented 发狂的, 精神错乱的
concealed 隐藏的, 隐瞒的

Answer the questions.

1. Why have almost all airports all over the world instituted pre-boarding security checks for weapons?
2. What is the point the agent must take about the search?

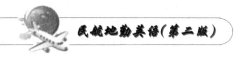

★ Further Reading 2

New EU Aviation Security Regulations

New EU aviation security regulations took effect on 6th November, 2006. From the 6th November only containers of 100 mls or less of liquids, gels, pastes, lotions and cosmetics may be brought through the passenger security screening points at all EU airports. In addition, these items MUST be presented at the passenger security screening point in a transparent re-sealable bag of no more than one litre capacity, 20 cm*20 cm.

The new rules apply to liquids such as water and other beverages, aerosol cans and toiletries such as toothpaste, shaving cream, hair gel, lip-gloss and creams. There are two exceptions to the rules—baby food and medicines needed during the flight.

Exempt items must also be placed in a separate transparent re-sealable bag and presented separately at the passenger security screening area.

So, from the 6th November the following rules apply to liquids in hand luggage:

1. Passengers can only take liquids, gels, pastes, lotions and cosmetics in containers of no more than 100 millilitres in size through the passenger security point at all EU airports.

2. These containers must be carried in a transparent, re-sealable plastic bag and presented separately to the security screening officers.

3. There is a limit of one transparent plastic bag per person.

4. The volume of the transparent plastic bag may not be greater than one litre, 20 cm*20 cm.

5. The transparent plastic bag must be re-sealable.

When passing through the passenger security point, a passenger must place the transparent re-sealable bag containing liquids, and other substances covered by the regulations, separately, in the tray for X-ray screening.

If a passenger must carry some liquids or other substances covered by the regulations in his hand luggage, he needs to pack them in the required transparent, re-sealable bag BEFORE HE SETS OUT ON HIS JOURNEY. These bags are available at most local supermarkets. However, during the introductory period, transparent plastic bags will be available at the airport.

★ Further Reading 3

New Rules for Taking Liquids through Security

To comply with the new guidelines recommended by the Hong Kong SAR Government, all departing flights from Hong Kong International Airport have to adopt new measures on hand baggage restrictions starting from March 21, 2007 (Wednesday).

New rules for taking liquids through security
旅客攜帶液體新規定（香港國際機場）

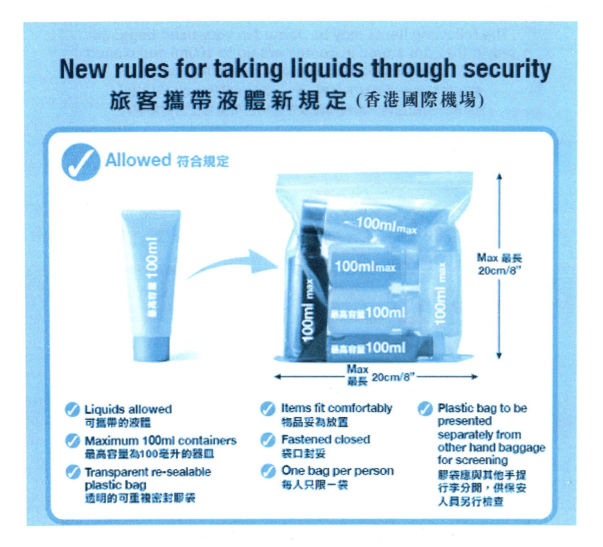

The following items may be carried in your hand baggage only if they are stored in containers up to 100ml and placed in a transparent re-sealable plastic bag.

旅客如要隨身攜帶以下物品，便必須將物品放置在容量不超過100毫升的器皿內，再將器皿放在透明的可重複密封的膠袋內。

- **Gels** 凝膠狀物品
  Examples: hair gel, shower gel
  例如：頭髮定形凝膠、洗澡液

- **Lotions and liquids** 乳液及液體
  Examples: sun cream, suntan oil, suntan spray, face cream, body lotion, roll-on deodorant, perfume, aftershave
  例如：防曬霜、防曬油、防曬噴霧、面霜、護膚乳液、走珠式香體劑、香水、鬚後水

- **Pastes** 膏狀物
  Examples: toothpaste, Vaseline, cream eye shadow
  例如：牙膏、凡士林、眼影膏

- **Pressurised foams and sprays** 壓縮泡沫及噴霧
  Examples: shaving foam, shower foam, tanning foam, pressurised deodorant
  例如：剃鬚泡沫、洗澡泡沫、防曬泡沫、壓縮香體劑

- **Foodstuffs** 食物
  Examples: water, soft drinks, yoghurt, soup, syrup
  例如：清水、汽水、乳酪、湯、糖漿

- **Liquid cosmetics** 液體化妝品
  Examples: liquid foundation, lip gloss, liquid mascara, make-up remover, nail polish
  例如：粉底液、唇彩、睫毛液、卸妝液、指甲油

★ Liquids in containers over 100ml must be packed into checked baggage.
液體如存放在容量超過100毫升器皿內，則必須放在寄艙行李內託運。

The following items are allowed in hand baggage.
以下物品可以隨身攜帶：

- **Medicines** 藥物
  Quantity essential for your trip.
  Example: diabetic kit
  只限旅程所須要數量，如糖尿病藥物包

- **Baby food** 嬰兒食品
  Quantity required for your trip (pastes and liquids)
  只限旅程所須要數量（糊狀及液體）

- **Non-liquid cosmetics** 非液體化妝品
  Examples: solid deodorant, lipstick, powder foundation
  例如：固體香體劑、唇膏、粉末狀粉底

★ Medicines, baby food and milk over 100ml must be presented for inspection at X-ray.
任何超過100毫升的藥物、嬰兒食品及牛奶，必須出示接受X光檢查。

The new rules are in accordance with the Civil Aviation Department regulations and in line with the International Civil Aviation Organisation guidelines.
以上保安措施符合民航處的規定，並配合國際民航組織的指引。

Unit 5

Associated Examinations in Airport

🔹 *Read the statements below and act as a customs officer at the airport with your partner.*

"There are two channels, red and green, in China customs. Take the red one if you have something to declare, otherwise the green one. If you are uncertain which channel you should take, then take the red one."

"If you take the red channel the customs officer will check to see whether you have to pay duty, deposit the items at Customs, or allow you to take them into China and take them out on your departure."

"If you take things such as computers, cameras, video cameras, gold and silver, printed or recorded materials, or anything more than you need during your travel in China, you have to fill in the 'Customs Luggage Declaration Form.' Similarly, if you are planning to leave any sort of significant item behind, you should also fill out the form."

"A copy of the form must be retained by the traveler and be submitted to Customs when leaving the country. All the items declared on the form must be brought out of China or else import duty will be charged on them."

VOCABULARY ASSISTANT

Customs 海关 channel 通道
declare 申报 retain 保存
submit 服从

Dialogue—The Customs at the Airport (1) 机场海关

Listen to the dialogue and fill out the blanks.

Setting: As Mr. Wright has nothing to declare, he goes through the green channel. The customs agent is inspecting him.

C: Good morning, sir. Are these your bags?
P: Yes, that's right.
C: 1_____?
P: No. I've only got clothes and things like that.
C: 2_____?

P: I'm here on business.

C: I see. 3_____?

P: Not at all.

C: 4_____?

P: Presents for some of my friends. They're Chinese glass vases.

C: 5_____?

P: I've got 100 cigarettes, but I haven't got any spirits.

C: 6_____?

P: Not at all. Here it is.

C: Right, that's all. Thank you.

VOCABULARY ASSISTANT

inspect 检查   purpose 目的
tobacco 烟草制品   cigarette 香烟
spirits 烈酒   perfume 香水
duty 税   confiscate 没收，充公

(Mrs. Wright has two bottles of perfume and she is asked to pay duty on them.)

C: 7_____?

P: Oh, yes. Here you are.

C: Well, this is quite a list, isn't it?

P: Yes. I put down everything. I wonder if you have noticed that I have two bottles of perfume listed in the declaration. 8_____?

C: Yes, I'm afraid so.

P: And what will the duty on the perfume be?

C: It will be 40 dollars.

P: Oh, goodness. That's almost as much as I paid for the perfume.

C: I'm sorry. But the duty on perfume is very high.

P: Supposing I don't pay that much duty.

C: Well, 9_____.

P: Oh, no. I think I'd better pay the duty. You see, it's my favorite perfume.

C: Even after you've paid the duty, I guess it's still cheaper than buying it locally.

P: Yes, I suppose so.

◆ Dialogue—The Customs at the Airport (2) 机场海关

Read the following dialogues with your partner and make up new dialogues by using the situations given below.

Setting: Mr. Jackson is invited to come to China by a Chinese company and his friend Mr. Wilson, who is a reporter for a newspaper in U.S.A., comes with him. They are going through the customs inspection.

C: May I see your passport, please?

P1: Certainly. Here it is.

69

C: You are here on business, I think?

P1: Yes. A Chinese company has invited me for business talk.

C: How long will you stay?

P1: Just one week.

C: How many pieces of baggage have you got?

P1: Two cases. In this case, I have a video camera. It's for my own use.

C: Do you intend to take it out on your departure?

P1: Yes, I do.

C: According to regulations, the video camera you've brought along for personal use can be passed for the time being duty free, but you will have to take it out with you when you leave the country.

P1: I will.

C: Well, have a good time in China.

P1: Thank you.

C: Hello, sir. Can you come and open your bag please. I have to inspect it.

P2: OK.

C: You have three cameras with you?

P2: Yes, I have. I'm a reporter for a newspaper, so I bring three different types of cameras with me to take pictures of China.

C: With articles of this kind you shouldn't go through the green channel, you should go through the red channel.

P: Why is that?

C: Passengers without anything to declare go through the green channel, and passengers who are just like you with something to declare should go through the red channel.

P: Oh, is it? I have to go through the red channel? But what do I do?

C: Please fill in this Customs Declaration Form, and keep it safe. When you depart, you have to hand it in for checking.

P: OK, thank you.

Make up your own dialogues according to the following situations.

1. Mr. Owen is flying back to America. He has bought one bottle of perfume and two watches for his friends. Now he is going through the Customs Inspection. A valuable watch is often one of the items that a passenger has to pay duty on. When Mr. Owen doesn't want to pay that much duty on the watch, what would you say to him?

2. Ms. Williams is not quite familiar with the customs formalities. If she has something to declare, what would you tell her to do?

Unit 5 Associated Examinations in Airport

Visitors are allowed to carry into China a limited quantity of duty-free goods including:

- 2 liters of alcoholic beverages
- 400 cigarettes
- 50 g (2 ounces) of gold or silver
- US$ less than 5000
- Chinese RMB with a total value less than 20,000 yuan
- Reasonable amount of perfume
- 1 still camera and reasonable amount of film

Match the two columns sentences and put them into right order to form a dialogue.

Agent

A: OK. Please open your luggage, and I'll tell you what you should declare.

B: How many bottles have you got with you?

C: Hello, madam. Have you anything to declare?

D: You should declare the video camera, the camera and the films. Do you have any alcohol?

E: See you. Have a good journey.

F: I'm sorry. According to the regulations, a passenger can only take 2 bottles on board the aircraft. So you can't take so many.

G: You may give them to your friends who come to see you off. This is the Customs Declaration Form. Please fill in it. And then you can go through the other formalities. Be sure to keep the form safe.

The right order for this dialogue is:

Passenger

a. All right, thank you. See you.

b. Oh, I don't know. This is my first time in China. I don't know what should be declared.

c. Six bottles.

d. All right. Here you are.

e. Yes, I have got some Beijing Erguotou. This is a special local product, so I want to take some back for my friends.

f. What shall I do with my 4 more bottles?

VOCABULARY ASSISTANT

special local product 特产
formality 手续
Customs Declaration Form
通关申报表格

Prohibited imports include: fresh fruit, arms, ammunition and explosives, printed matter, films or tapes "detrimental to China", narcotic drugs, animals and plants.

Remember: All the receipts of the valuable articles, such as jewelry, jade, gold and silver ornaments, handicrafts, artifacts, paintings and calligraphy, you bought in China should be kept for the exit check. Antiques are not permitted to leave China without the proper "Certificates for the Export of Cultural Relics" from the Chinese Authorities.

Information Bank

世界海关组织

世界海关组织 (World Customs Organization, WCO)，其前身为海关合作理事会 (Customs Cooperation Council, CCC),是国际性的海关组织,也是世界性的,为统一关税、简化海关手续而建立的政府间协调组织。

世界海关组织的宗旨是：研究有关关税合作问题,审议征税技术及其经济因素以统一关税,简化海关手续,确保对其他两个公约的统一解释和应用。监督各国的执行情况,负责调解纠纷,并向成员国提供有关关税、条例和手续方面的情报和咨询。

世界海关组织现有成员161个，来自世界各大洲，代表不同的社会经济发展水平,通过政策协调和合作帮助各个成员实现其确定的经济发展目标。我国于1983年7月18日加入世界海关组织。

20世纪70年代初该组织研究并制订了《商品名称及编码协调制度》,简称《协调制度》(Harmonized System, HS)。现有150多个国家和地区实行HS编码,1992年1月1日我国海关正式采用HS编制中国的海关商品编码。

Unit 5 Associated Examinations in Airport

✚ Read the following statements below and get familiar with the regulations and formalities.

"Good morning, this is the Quarantine Inspection of China sector. Please fill in the Quarantine Declaration Form according to the items on the card: name, sex, nationality, passport number and the countries and cities where you have stayed within the last 4 weeks. The most important is to fill in the country or region where you have come from. Please mark the following symptoms or illnesses you have now, and the items of food and plants that you are bringing into China. Finally, please don't forget to sign your name. Thank you."

VOCABULARY ASSISTANT

quarantine 检疫   nationality 国籍
region 地区   mark 做标记
symptom 症状   diarrhea 痢疾、腹泻
jaundice 黄疸   vomit 呕吐
tuberculosis 肺结核   medication 药物治疗

Health Check: Those who enter China are required to fill out a Health Declaration Form issued by the inspection and quarantine authorities. Those who came from yellow-fever infected areas must show valid vaccination certificates to the inspection and quarantine authorities. Those who suffer from fever, diarrhea, skin diseases, jaundice, vomiting, AIDS/HIV infection, VD (venereal disease) and tuberculosis are required to declare this information. Medications and other special goods should be declared and are subject to inspection.

73

Inspection and Quarantine Information for Entry into China

1. Blood and blood products.
2. Fruits, peppers, eggplant and tomatoes.
3. Animal carcasses and specimen.
4. Soil.
5. Pathogens, pests and other harmful organisms.
6. Live animals (except cats and dogs as pets).
7. Animal parts and products including eggs, raw hides, skin, hair, hoofs, fat, meat (including viscera), fresh milk, cheese, butter, cream, whey powder, blood and blood products; silkworm pupa and aquatic plants and animal products.
8. Genetic materials including semen, zygotes and embryos.
9. Waste materials and soiled or dirty clothing.

HEALTH DECLARATION FORM ON ENTRY/EXIT

Entry-Exit Inspection and Quarantine of the P. R. China

Notice: For your and others' health, please fill in the form truly and completely. False information of intent will be followed with legal consequences.

Name_____ Sex: □Male □Female

Date of Birth_____ Nationality/Region_____

Passport No._____ Flight No._____

The contact address and telephone number_____
_____

1. Have you had close contact with poultry or bird in the past 7 days?
   Yes□ No□
2. Have you had close contact with patients or suspects suffering from Avian Influenza in the past 7 days? Yes□ No□
3. Please mark the symptoms and diseases you have with "√" in the corresponding "□".
   □Fever □Snivel □Cough □Sore throat
   □Headache □Diarrhoea □Vomiting □Breath Difficulty
   □Venereal disease □AIDS/HIV □Psychosis
   □Active pulmonary tuberculosis

I declare all the information given in this form are true and correct.

Signature:_____ Date:_____

Temperature (for quarantine official only):_____℃

Dialogue—At the Airport Quarantine Inspection of China Sector 机场检验检疫

Read the following dialogues and finish the exercises below.

C: Hello, please give me the card you have filled in.
P: Here you are.
C: Did you come from Kenya?
P: Yes, I came from Kenya.
C: Oh, can you show me your vaccination certificate, please?
P: Just a moment. Here you are.
C: Oh, I'm sorry. The yellow fever vaccination is not valid any longer in your certificate.
P: Is it not? Well, what shall I do now?

> **VOCABULARY ASSISTANT**
>
> Kenya 肯尼亚   vaccination 接种疫苗
> certificate 证书   yellow fever 黄热病
> not...any longer 不再   valid 有效的
> infirmary 医务室

Unit 5 Associated Examinations in Airport

C: You will have to take the vaccination against yellow fever here.
P: Oh, where shall I take the vaccination?
C: Please follow that person. She will take you to the vaccination infirmary.
P: Thank you.

C: Hello, please follow me to have your injection in the infirmary.
P: OK.
C: Please take off your coat and roll up your sleeve.
P: Is it painful?
C: A little. But if you relax your muscles, the pain will be milder.
P: I'm very afraid of pain. Could I have a smaller dose?
C: Well, the dose is defined. And a smaller amount won't be so effective.
P: Oh, I see.
C: OK, let me rub it with cotton wool.
P: Finished?
C: Yes, please hold the cotton wool on your arm for a while. And please pay RMB 60 for the vaccination.
P: All right, thank you. Here you are.
C: Here is your receipt. Bye.
P: Bye-bye.

VOCABULARY ASSISTANT

injection 注射   roll up 卷起   sleeve 袖子
dose 剂量   effective 有效的,起作用的
receipt 收据

Make up your own dialogues according to the following situations.

1. Mr. Gladstone who came from Sri Lanka arrives at the Quarantine Inspection of the airport, but his yellow fever vaccination is no longer valid in his vaccination certificate.
2. Ms. Muller who came from Indonesia wants to know how to fill in the Quarantine Declaration Form.

Translate the following sentences into Chinese.

1. If you are carrying any objects, such as any fruits, peppers, eggplants, and tomatoes; animal carcasses and specimens; soil; waste and used clothes, please hand them over to the Quarantine

75

Inspection officials or dispose of them into the quarantine bin.

2. According to our regulations, human blood and its products are prohibited from being carried into China.

Read the statements below and get familiar with the regulations and formalities.

The following personnel are prohibited from entering China:
1. People who have broken Chinese laws and others who were expelled and have not been permitted to re-enter China.
2. Known or suspected terrorists and those who engage in violent and subversive activities.
3. Known or suspected dealers in contraband, drug trade, or prostitution.
4. People who suffer from Hansen's disease (leprosy), AIDS/HIV, VD (venereal disease), pulmonary tuberculosis and other infectious diseases.
5. People who cannot afford the cost of their stay in China.
6. People who are known or suspected to engage in activities that are harmful to China's social order and national security.
7. Those who do not hold valid passports, visas and other credentials.
8. Those who hold stolen, forged or altered passports, visas and credentials.
9. Those who refuse to have their credentials and documents checked.
10. Those who are forbidden to enter China by the Ministry of Public Security of China and the Ministry of State Security.

Ladies and gentlemen, here is the place to have your passports checked. Please stand in lines before the Check Desks No. 1, 2, 3 and 4. Please have your passports and completed entry cards ready. Those who have no entry cards may come here and get one. Please follow the introductions on the form. Fill in each item, such as name, nationality, date of birth, number and type of your passport and so on. Please fill in the form using a pen or ball-pen. After you've finished it, please hand it to the inspector inside the check desk together with your passport. Thank you for your cooperation.

Unit 5 Associated Examinations in Airport

Card Sample

DEPARTURE CARD 外国人出境卡
For Immigration clearance 请交边防检查官员查验

- Family name 姓
- Given names 名
- Passport No. 护照号码
- Date of birth 出生日期 Year 年 Month 月 Day 日
- Flight No./Ship's name/Train No. 航班号/船名/车次
- Nationality 国籍
- Male 男 □ Female 女 □

签名 Signature
以上申明真实准确。
I hereby declare that the statement given above is true and accurate.

要妥善保留此卡，如遗失将会对出境造成不便。
Retain this card in your possession, failure to do so may delay your departure from China.
请注意背面重要提示。See the back →

ARRIVAL CARD 外国人入境卡
For Immigration clearance 请交边防检查官员查验

- Family name 姓
- Given names 名
- Passport No. 护照号码
- Nationality 国籍
- Intended Address in China 在华住址
- Date of birth 出生日期 Year 年 Month 月 Day 日
- Visa No. 签证号码
- Place of Visa issuance 签证签发地
- Flight No./Ship's name/Train No. 航班号/船名/车次
- Male 男 □ Female 女 □

Purpose of visit (one only) 入境事由 (只能填写一项)
- Conference/Business 会议/商务 □
- Visiting friends or relatives 探亲访友 □
- Return home 返回常住地 □
- Visit 访问 □
- Employment 就业 □
- Settle down 定居 □
- Sightseeing in leisure 观光/休闲 □
- Study 学习 □
- others 其他 □

以上申明真实准确。
I hereby declare that the statement given above is true and accurate.
签名 Signature

Important Notice

1. Aliens who do not lodge at hotels, guesthouses or inns shall, within 24 hours (72 hours in rural areas) of entry, go through accommodation registration at local police station.
2. Aliens holding visas Z, X or J-1 shall, within 30 days of entry, apply for Residence Permits to the exit-entry department of the public security bureau of the city where the applicants reside.
3. Aliens shall not be employed in China without permission of the competent authorities of the Chinese Government.
4. Aliens who reside or stay in China shall carry with themselves their passports or Residence Permits for possible examination.
5. In case of emergency, please dial 110 to seek help from police.

Dialogue—At the Frontier Inspection 边防检查

Setting: Mr. and Mrs. Williams with their son are at the Check-in Desk in Immigration Hall at the airport.

C: Morning, madam. Please show me your 1_____.

P1: Here you are.

C: How many kids do you have with you?

P1: Only one. His name is on my passport.

C: But his name is 2_____, why?

P1: Really? Sorry, I have no idea about the reason. I had 3_____ both of us. 4_____, I thought everything was OK.

C: Please wait for a moment. We'll investigate it, and be back at once.

C: Hello, sir. May I see your passport, please?

P2: Here you are.

C: Do you come to China alone?

P2: No, my wife and my son are with me to 5_____.

C: You come here just to tour in Beijing only?

P2: Not exactly. We come to Beijing but we'd like to visit Shanghai as well.

C: I see. Have you 6_____ the entry cards?

P2: Yes, I have. Have you looked at them?

C: Yes, but I should mention one thing, 7_____.

P2: Yes, I know. But I didn't think of it until we left New York.

C: Then, you are going back to New York, aren't you?

P2: Yes, that's true. 8_____. Thank you.

C: You are welcome. 9_____.

P2: Thank you. Bye.

VOCABULARY ASSISTANT

Immigration Hall 入境大厅　　passport 护照

visa 签证　　tour 旅行　　entry card 入境卡

expire 期满　　renew 更新

★ Further Reading 1

Introduction to Chinese Visa

A Chinese visa is a permit issued by the Chinese visa authorities to an alien for entry into, exit from or transit through China. The Chinese visa authorities may issue a Diplomatic, Courtesy, Service or Ordinary Visa to an alien according to his status, purpose of visit to China or passport type. The Ordinary Visa consists of eight sub-categories, which are respectively marked with Chinese phonetic letters D, F, G, L, X and Z.

- Tourist (L) Visa is issued to an alien who comes to China temporarily for tourism, sightseeing, visits with friends or relatives, medical treatment or other private purposes. China tourist visa is valid for 6 months with single-entry, or 6 months with double-entry, or 6 months/12 months with multiple-entry.
- Business (F) Visa is issued to an alien who is invited to China for a business visit, research, lecture, scientific/technological and cultural exchanges, attending professional or business convention, or short-term studies for a period of no more than six months. China business visa is valid for 6 months with single-entry, 6 months with double-entry, or 6 months/12 months with multiple-entry.
- Work (Z) Visa is issued to foreigners who enter China for a post or employment (such as teacher), and their accompanying family members. The holder of a work visa shall go through residential formalities in the local public security department within thirty days of entry into China.
- Study (X) Visa is issued to an alien who comes to China for study, advanced studies or intern practice for a period of more than six months. If the study period is no more than six months, then the applicant shall apply for a business visa (type F).
- Transit (G) Visa is issued to aliens transit through China. U.S. passport holders must obtain a transit visa to transit through all Chinese airports except Pudong International Airport in Shanghai.
- Resident (D) Visa is issued to an alien who goes to reside permanently in China.
  Visas are not required of aliens, who hold final destination tickets and have booked seats on international airliners flying directly through China, and will stay in a transit city for less than 24 hours without leaving the airport.

Visas are not required of Citizens of the following countries, who transit through Pudong Airport or Hongqiao Airport of Shanghai, provided they hold valid passports, visas for the onward countries, final destination tickets and have booked seats, and stay in Shanghai for less than 48 hours: Republic of Korea, the United States, Canada, Australia, New Zealand, Germany, France, Netherlands, Belgium, Luxemburg, Portugal, Spain, Italy, Austria, Greece.

No visa is required for ordinary passport holders from Singapore, Brunei and Japan to visit China for up to 15 days for business, sightseeing, visiting relatives and friends or transit.

VOCABULARY ASSISTANT

entry 入境	exit 出境	transit 过境
Diplomatic Visa 外交签证	Courtesy Visa 礼遇签证	Service Visa 公务签证
Ordinary Visa 普通签证	sub-categories 子种类	phonetic letter 拼音字母
temporarily 暂时地	single-entry 一次入境	double-entry 二次入境
multiple-entry 多次入境	accompanying 偕行的	intern 实习
permanently 永久地	provided 假设、倘若	Republic of Korea 韩国
Netherlands 荷兰	Belgium 比利时	Luxemburg 卢森堡
Portugal 葡萄牙	Brunei 文莱	

Answer the questions according to the above text.

1. If you are a manager in a company and invited to take part in an exhibition which will last for 1 month in the United States, which kind of visa do you need to apply for?
2. If you are invited to attend your best friend's wedding ceremony in Japan, which type of visa do you need to apply for?

Information Bank

什么是签证？

签证（Visa）是一国政府主管机关依照法律规章为申请入、出境和过境的外国人颁发的一种书面许可证明。通常是附载于申请人所持的护照或其他国际旅行证件上。在特殊情况下，凭有效护照或其他国际旅行证件可做在另纸上。有些国家对出入国境的本国公民也颁发签证。

签证的种类

外交签证（Dipomatic Visa）是一国政府主管机关依法为进入或经过该国国境应当给予外交特权和豁免的人员所颁发的签证。外交签证一般发给持外交护照人员。签证颁发国依据本国法规和国际惯例，给予持证人相应的方便、优遇、特权和豁免。

公务签证（Service Visa）是一国政府主管机关依法为进入或该国国境应当给予公务人员待遇的人士所颁发的签证。有的国家将该种签证称为官员签证（Official Visa）。公务签证一般发给持公务护照人员。

Unit 5　Associated examinations in Airport

礼遇签证(Courtesy Visa)是一些国家政府主管机关依法为进入或经过该国国境应当给予相应礼遇的人员所颁发的签证。这些人一般是身份高但又未持有外交护照的人员或已卸任的外国党政高级官员及知名人士。签证颁发国根据本国法规和国际惯例,给予持证人应有的尊重和礼遇。

普通签证(General Visa)是一国政府主管机关依法为进入或经过该国国境应当给予普通人员待遇的人士所颁发的签证。普通签证一般发给持普通护照或其他有效的国际旅行证件的人员。

★ **Further Reading 2**

Introduction to Chinese Passports

Passports of the People's Republic of China are issued to Chinese citizens as certificates to prove their nationality and identity for the purposes of entering or exiting Chinese border and traveling or residing in foreign countries.

Passports of the PRC are classified into Diplomatic Passport, Service Passport, Ordinary Passport, Hong Kong Special Administrative Region Passport and Macao Special Administrative Region Passport. Ordinary Passport is further composed of Ordinary Passport for Public Affairs and Ordinary Passport for Private Affairs.

The maximum validity of Diplomatic Passport, Service Passports and Ordinary Passport is 5 years. All these passports can be renewed before the expiry date. The validity period of Hong Kong SAR Passport is 10 years. Hong Kong SAR Passport issued to those under the age of 16 years shall be valid for 5 years. The validity of the Macao SAR passport is 10 years. Macao SAR passport issued to those under the age of 18 years shall be valid for 5 years.

Diplomatic Passport is principally issued to senior officials of the Communist Party, the government, and the People's Liberation Army, principal leaders of the National People's Congress, the Chinese Peoples' Political Consultative Conference, and all democratic parties, diplomats, consular officers and their accompanying spouses, underage children, diplomatic couriers, etc. Service Passport is principally issued to officials ranked as division chief and above of governmental offices, staff members of diplomatic and consular missions in foreign countries, the United Nations' organizations and its specialized agencies, and their accompanying spouses and underage children, etc.

Ordinary Passport for Public Affairs is principally issued to staff in the governmental offices at all levels and to employees of state-owned enterprises or institutions.

Ordinary Passport for private affairs is principally issued to overseas Chinese and those who go abroad for personal affairs, such as residing, visiting friends or relatives, inheriting properties, studying, working, or sightseeing, etc.

Hong Kong SAR Passports are issued to Chinese citizens who hold permanent identity cards of Hong Kong.

Macao SAR Passports are issued to Chinese citizens who are permanent residents of the Macao SAR.

VOCABULARY ASSISTANT

nationality 国籍
identity 身份
border 边界、国界
reside in 居住
Diplomatic Passport 外交护照
Service Passport 公务护照
Ordinary Passport 普通护照
principally adv. 主要地

Hong Kong Special Administrative Region Passport
香港特别行政区护照
Macao Special Administrative Region Passport
澳门特别行政区护照
Ordinary Passport for Public Affairs
因公普通护照
Ordinary Passport for Private Affairs
因私普通护照

Answer the questions according to the text above.

1. If you were going to study in Singapore, which type of passport do you need to apply for?
2. If you were the wife of an diplomat, you need to accompany your husband working in Indonesia, which kind of passport do you need to apply for?

Information Bank

护照的种类

我国的护照分为外交护照、公务护照和普通护照。普通护照又分因公普通护照和因私普通护照。

外交护照主要发给副部长、副省长等以上的中国政府官员,党、政、军等重要代表团正、副团长以及外交官员、领事官员及其随行配偶、未成年子女、外交信使等。公务护照主要发给中国各级政府部门的工作人员、中国驻外国的外交代表机关、领事机关和驻联合国组织系统及其有关专门机构的工作人员及其随行配偶、未成年子女等。

因公普通护照主要发给中国国营企业、事业单位出国从事经济、贸易、文化、体育、卫生、科学技术交流等公务活动的人员、公派留学、进修人员、访问学者及公派出国从事劳务的人员等。

因私普通护照发给定居、探亲、访友、继承遗产、自费留学、就业、旅游和其他因私人事务出国和定居国外的中国公民。护照的内容主要包括姓名、出生地、性别、发照日期、有效期等,护照均应贴有持照人的照片。

Unit 6

Service for Special Passengers

✥ *Discussion: What are the special requests and needs that passengers have? As a clerk, how do you assist your passengers to solve their difficulties?*

Passengers with child/children

Unaccompanied minors

Passengers with physical difficulties

VIP

Pregnant women

Check-in for Passengers with Children

Dialogue—Check-in for Passengers with Children. 带小孩的旅客办理登记

C: Hello, madam.

P: Hello.

C: How many pieces of luggage will you be checking in today?

P: I'm checking in two. Can I bring the buggy with me or do I have to check it in?

C: You can take it with you. It will be taken from you before you get on the plane and will be given back to you at the door of the plane when you arrive at your destination. OK?

P: OK. Thanks. Can I have the emergency exit seats please, so that there is more room for my daughter and I?

C: Sorry, madam, that's not allowed because you are traveling with an infant. Anyone wants to seat near the emergency exit has to be over 18 years old.

P: Ah, I see. Well, are there any other seats with more room?

C: I can seat you in the middle seat of the first row where there is plenty room.

P: Thank you very much.

C: Have you got anything sharp in your carry-on bag? Such as a scissors, eyebrow tweezers, baby pins or needles?

P: No, I haven't.

C: Great. So here is your boarding card, and you will be boarding through Gate 15 at 3:30.

P: Thank you.

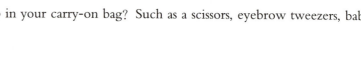

VOCABULARY ASSISTANT

buggy 婴儿车   emergency exit 紧急出口   infant 婴儿
sharp 尖的   eyebrow tweezers 眉毛夹   pin 别针
needle 针

Unit 6 Service for Special Passengers

Check-in for Unaccompanied Children

🛬 *What are unaccompanied children and what are the airline rules for them? Listen to the following passage and try to get the answer to these two questions.*

Most airlines allow 1_____ to fly, though usually with several restrictions. Programs vary widely from airline to airline, and no two airlines will have the same polices. This brief overview will discuss the 2_____ of these programs as well as a number of issues that you may want to address before allowing a child to travel unaccompanied.

While a child 3_____ is considered an unaccompanied child by the airlines, a group of children would be considered unaccompanied if there is not 4_____ traveling with them.

Most airlines have a minimum age for unaccompanied children, typically 5_____, and a maximum age, typically 6_____. You or your child may be asked to provide some kind of 7_____ of the child's age, so be prepared to bring appropriate documentation to the airport.

For unaccompanied children traveling under the airline's supervision, there may be additional restrictions and requirements. Typical requirements and restrictions may include the following:

- Allowing unaccompanied children only on 8_____
- Having a 9_____ if the child is on a flight requiring a change of aircraft or a change of flight number
- Not allowing unaccompanied children on 10_____ of the day for that destination
- Not allowing unaccompanied children on flights that involve a second carrier
- Requiring earlier check in, typically 11_____ minutes before departure
- Charging adult 12_____ associated with the service for unaccompanied children

VOCABULARY ASSISTANT		
uncompanied 无人伴随的	restriction 规定	policy 政策
issue 问题	proof 证明	minimum 最低的
maximum 最高的	supervision 监督、管理	

Dialogue—Check-in for Unaccompanied Children (1) 无陪伴儿童办理登机(1)

C: Hello. May I have your tickets and passport?

P: I'm checking in for my daughter.

C: OK, and how old is she?

P: She is ten years old.

C: OK. You will have to fill in a form with details, such as contact number, address, where she is traveling to, and the details of the person who is going to pick her at the airport.

P: OK.

C: Here's the form.

P: Thank you.

Some minutes later

C: She will be seated in Row 1C, and aisle seat. I will put a note into the computer that she is traveling alone.

P: Thank you.

C: Will she be checking in any luggage?

P: Yes, just a small suitcase.

C: Would you mind placing it on the belt, please?

P: Here's the form.

C: The copy is for your daughter to hold onto. Make sure it's kept somewhere safe.

P: Where will she be boarding?

C: Through Gate 7 at 8:25.

P: Thank you so much.

C: It's a pleasure.

Read the above dialogue carefully and discuss the following question with a partner. Then make up short dialogues by reference to the language expressions in the boxes.

How would you help an adult to check in for his or her child who is traveling unaccompanied?

◎ May I have his/her tickets and passport?

◎ You will have to fill in a form with details, such as...

◎ I'd like to let you know that we'll seat him/her in...

◎ Will he/she be checking in any luggage?

◎ The copy is for him/her to hold onto. Make sure it's kept somewhere safe.

Unit 6 Service for Special Passengers

Dialogue—Check-in for Unaccompanied Children （2）无陪伴儿童办理登机(2)

C: Excuse me, ma'am. I'd like to let you know that we'll seat Li Xiang in a forward row so that he will be easy for our flight attendants to find and watch.

P: You are so thoughtful. Thank you very much.

C: We have prepared an envelope to contain his travel documents. As Li Xiang's guardian, could you please read carefully and complete the form on the cover of the envelope?

...

P: Here you are. Is that all right?

C: Yes, perfect. Thank you. This is your copy. I'll put his passport, ticket and other travel documents in the envelope and pass it to our senior flight attendant on his flight.

P: Be sure that your flight attendants will watch him on board.

C: Yes. Here is a badge for an unaccompanied child. （To Li Xiang）Let me pin this badge on your chest so that our flight attendants can identify you and look after you during the flight. （To the guardian）He will soon be escorted to the cabin crew.

P: Is there anyone to assist him through Immigration and Customs after deplaning at San Francisco Airport?

C: Yes, our ground staff at the airport will be informed of his arrival beforehand and will be ready to meet him.

VOCABULARY ASSISTANT

guardian 监护人   cover 封面   senior flight attendant 乘务长
badge 标签   identify 识别出   escort 伴随   assist 帮助
deplane 下飞机   ground staff 地勤人员   inform 通知

Information Bank—Unaccompanied Minor Requested for Carriage-Handling Advice.

无成人陪伴儿童乘机申请书
UNACCOMPANIED MINOR REQUESTED FOR CARRIAGE-HANDLING ADVICE

日期(DATE):

至(To)   售票服务处(OFFICE CEA)
儿童姓名(NAME OF MINOR):   年龄(AGE):_____
(包括儿童乳名–INCLUDING NICKNAME)   性别(SEX):_____
航程(ROUTING)

航班号 FLT NO	日期 DATE	自 FROM	至 TO

航站 STATION	接送人姓名 NAME OF PERSON ACCOMPANYING	地址、电话号码 ADDRESS AND TEL NO.
始发站 ON DEPARTURE		
中途分程站 STOPOVER POINT		
中途分程站 STOPOVER POINT		
到达站 ON ARRIVAL		

儿童父母或监护人姓名、地址、电话号码
PARENT/GUARDIAN–NAME, ADDRESS AND TEL NO.:_____

申请人签字(Signature):_____   经办人签字(Clerk):_____

Unit 6 Service for Special Passengers

✚ **Complete the following dialogue and practice with your partner.**

C: Afternoon, madam. May I see your travel documents?

P: Sure. Here you are. But they are not for me, for this little boy.

C: Jim. Is he your son, traveling unaccompained?

P: I'm his aunt. He will be traveling alone, so we need your help, escorting him through Customs to his detination.

C: Sure. Now let me see the travel documents he needs. Passport, ticket...

P: And here is a form, Unaccompanied Monor Requested for Carriage-Handling Advice.

C: 1_____? （谁到机场来接他？）

P: His parents, of course. I've already informed them of the flight schedule.

C: Good. Everything is in order. 2_____. （我给他安排在了第一排，这样我们机组的乘务员就能方便地照顾到他了。）

P: You are so thoughtful. Thank you very much indeed.

C: We have prepared an envelope to contain his travel documents. 3_____? （作为他的监护人，您能仔细地阅读一下无成人伴随儿童乘机表并填写这封皮上的内容吗？）

P: Here you are. Is that all right?

C: Yes, perfect. Thank you. 4_____. （我会把他的护照、机票和其他的文件放到信封里并交给他所乘飞机的乘务长。）During the flight he will be carrying this envelope on his chest so that our fight attendants can easily identity and look after him. Wait a moment please. He'll soon be escorted to the cabin crew.

P: Is there anyone to assist him through Immigration and Customs after deplaning?

C: Yes, 5_____. （机场的地勤人员会提前得知他将要到港的信息。）When he arrives he will be escorted through arrival formalities and then to meet his parent there.

◆ Who will come to meet him/her at the airport?

◆ You will have to fill in a form with details, such as contact number, address, where he/she is traveling, and the details of the person who is going to pick him/her up at the airport.

◆ He/She will be seated in Row 1C, an aisle seat. I will put a note into the computer that he/she is traveling alone.

◆ The copy is for your ... to hold onto. Make sure it's kept somewhere safe.

◆ We'll seat ... in a forward row so that he/she will be easy for our flight attendants to find and watch.

◆ We have prepared an envelope to contain his/her travel documents. As ...'s guardian,

could you please read carefully and complete the form on the cover of the envelope?
- ◆ I'll put his/her passport, ticket and other travel documents in the envelope and pass it to our senior flight attendant on his flight.
- ◆ Here is a badge for an unaccompanied child. Let me pin this badge on his/her chest so that our flight attendants can identify him/her and look after him/her during the flight.
- ◆ Our ground staff at the airport will be informed of his/her arrival beforehand and will be ready to meet him/her.

Read the following useful sentences.

Read the dialogues above carefully and make a similar one with your partner according to the given situation.

Mr. Sun takes his 7-year-old daughter, Lucy to the airport for check-in. Lucy will be travelling to New York unaccompanied. Lucy's grandmother will be meeting her at the airport.

Check-in for Passengers with Physical Difficulties

Dialogue—Check-in for Disabled Passengers 残障乘客办理登机

C: Good morning, sir.
P: Good morning.
C: Just yourself, sir?
P: No, I'm here for my friend. He is disabled and blind, and needs special assistance.
C: That won't be a problem, sir. May I have his ticket and passport, please?
P: Yes, here you are. He will need to be lifted on and off the plane.
C: Yes, I will get everything sorted out for him. Don't worry, sir.
P: Thank you.
C: How many bags is the gentleman checking in?
P: He's not checking in any; he has just a hand luggage.
C: Just the one piece?
P: Yes, just one.
C: He will be seated on 1st Row A2, an individual seat.

Unit 6 *Service for Special Passengers*

P: Is it Ok?

C: That's fine.

P: There will be somebody to bring him down to the gate. He then will be lifted onto the plane, and there will be someone to help him off as well. No worries, here is his boarding card and passport. Please wait on the side.

C: Thank you.

VOCABULARY ASSISTANT
sort 整理   individual 单独的

Listen to the dialogue and complete the blanks.

C: Miss, 1_____?

P: No, thank you just the same. My son has come to see me off and he will assist me.

C: I'm afraid he is not allowed to enter Immigration and Customs areas because 2_____.

P: Oh, I didn't think of that. Then, I will need your special assistance.

C: 3_____ if you would like one.

P: Yes, I would.

C: Miss, our agent will meet you at 4_____ just over there at 11:00 a.m., one hour before flight departure. The agent will be wearing a uniform like mine. He will 5_____.

P: Thank you.

Language Practice.

Setting: Different airlines offer different facilities for passengers who have got special needs. Suppose you are an agent of the following airline companies and introduce these special facilities your company provides for them.

London Heathrow Airport

All terminals offer:
- Ramps
- Wider access pathways
- Telephones at a height accessible to wheelchair users
- Disabled toilet facilities
- Reserved seating for disabled people in check-in areas

91

For general advice and information regarding the special needs facilities at Heathrow Airport telephone +44(0)870 000 0123.

Travel-Care is an independent agency offering assistance to anyone at London Heathrow Airport who has a problem. Travel-Care can be found in the Queens Building inbetween Terminals 1 and 2.
Open from Monday to Friday from 09.00~17.00 and closed Saturday/Sunday and Bank Holidays.
Telephone: +44(0)208 745 7495

Manchester Airport

The airport offers:
- A wide cross-section of staff have received training in sign language.
- Inductive coupler system built into all public telephones.
- Signs to assist passengers who may be deaf or hard of hearing.
- Special vehicles are provided to convey non-walking passengers and their companion and/or attendant.
- Designated parking facilities, adjacent to lifts, are available in the multi-storey car parks at all three terminals.
- Ramps and lifts are provided throughout the Airport. All lifts have tactile buttons and voice synthesisers.
- Telephones with good accessibility for wheelchair users are available throughout all three terminals. A public text payphone is situated in Terminal 1 International Arrivals.
- Specially designed toilets can be found in most areas of both terminal buildings and are clearly signposted.

Information Bank

Tips for Disabled Air Passengers

You should compare the arrangements offered by different airlines before making your booking and be sure to check whether the cost of any special assistance is included

Unit 6 Service for Special Passengers

in the price of your ticket.

Inform your airline of your particular needs in good time and check the policy of your airline if you wish to remain in your own wheelchair to the aircraft door rather than transfer to an airline wheelchair at check-in.

Remember that there are often long walking distances within airports and that this may cause you to require assistance. Pre-arranging any necessary assistance will ensure that it's available and that no time is lost in waiting for it to be arranged once you arrive at the airport.

Check-in for Other Special Passengers

Dialogue—Check-in for a VIP 贵宾办理登机手续

C: Mr. Willson, may I invite you to our VIP Lounge where you can relax until your flight is ready for boarding?

P: Thank you.

C: It is located in the departure hall near your boarding gate. This is Miss Yan, who will escort you there. If there is anything else we can do for you, please don't hesitate. We are at your service.

VOCABULARY ASSISTANT

lounge（配有沙发的）休息厅
relax 放松　　　hesitate 犹豫

Advice to Them

Give advice to pregnant passengers:

While air travel does not usually cause problems during pregnancy unless delivery is expected

within 14 days or less, in some cases, traveling by air has been known to cause complications or premature labor. Female Customers at any stage of pregnancy should consult with their physicians prior to air travel. Southwest Airlines strongly recommends against air travel after the 38th week of pregnancy. Depending on their physical condition, strength, and agility, pregnant women may, in some cases, be asked not to sit in an emergency exit seat.

Give advice to elderly passengers:

Step 1: Consider any health problems or issues. It is a good idea to mention travel plans to the elderly person's physician just to address any concerns or recommendations.

Step 2: Check the age requirement for senior discounts with your airline carrier. If your travel companion is over the age of 65, they may qualify for a discounted ticket fare. Check the other fares as well, as the specials are sometimes cheaper than the senior discount.

Step 3: Pack a light carry-on bag that contains a snack, a bottle of water and a two to three day supply of medication. Airlines don't offer the meal options they used to.

Step 4: Request any additional assistance that may be needed upon arrival. If a wheelchair or attendant will be needed, they can note this on the reservation to ensure aiport staff is adequate.

Step 5: Consider the travel times. Your elderly passenger may do better on a less crowded flight. If your travel plans are flexible, consider traveling during the middle of the day or mid-week when the airport is generally less crowded.

Step 6: Allow yourself plenty of time for the arrival and check-in process. Many senior fares require check-in at the ticket counter to show proof of age. Keep the boarding pass and proof of identification handy for the security check points.

Step 7: Take a few extra minutes to eat something, take any medication and go to the restroom once you have passed through security.

Step 8: Check to see if the airline allows early boarding. The boarding process usually begins 30 minutes prior to scheduled take-off. Most airlines will allow a passenger needing any special assistance to board the plane first regardless of ticket class or seating. This will help avoid standing in a long line to board and give you time to get comfortable before the plane is filled with other passengers.

Step 9: Drink plenty of water as the airplane air system can easily make you dehydrated. Make routine trips to the restroom even if it is just for movement, especially on longer flights.

★ Further Reading 1

Airlines' Assistance to Special Passengers

Airlines extend all possible to passengers who have special requests and needs. Everyday requests range from passengers wishing to transport a pet to others with special meal requirements.

Other passengers may require assistance with boarding a plane and getting seated due to a medical problem. Young passengers might require escorting around the airport or while on board, especially if they are traveling for the first time and are unfamiliar with procedures.

It is usually the agent's responsibility to communicate the passenger's request to the carrier. In more complex situations the agent may be required to deal directly with the airline on the customer's behalf, to make the necessary arrangements regarding the passenger's comfort and safety. The agent will format such requests by using special service request commands. Then he will send automated messages in a PNR. The airlines will then read them and respond, confirming or rejecting the request.

For more complicated requests, many agents find it simpler to telephone the carrier and talk directly to airline reservation staff.

The following describes a selection of special passenger categories.

Infants/babies

A baby is defined by most airlines as a child who has not yet had a second birthday. A child is defined as being between the ages of 2 and 12. After their twelfth birthdays, children are considered adult passengers and no longer qualify for reduced fares.

Babies are not always entitled to a seat, and must be accompanied by an adult. If two children under the age of two are traveling with one adult, a seat must usually be purchased and a child fare paid.

Most airlines will arrange for baby baskets to be available, especially on longer flights. Baskets should be arranged in advance. Baby food can also be orderd in advance. Special life jackets and safety belts for infants are available on board each aircraft.

Child Passengers

Referred to as unaccompained minors. These are children (usually under the age of 12) who, by arrangement, are traveling alone. The age at which a child traveling alone is accepted by an airline, and the procedures applying to UNMPs, vary from airline to airline.

A special UM form should normally be obtained and filled out. This provides the carrier with the name and contact for a

responsible adult. The person collecting the child at the destination then signs the same form. During the rest of the travel time a member of either the airport ground staff or the crew will accompany the child.

Pregnant Women

Pregnant women are advised to consult their doctor before traveling. A doctor's letter may be required by some airlines. Traveling in the early stages of a normal pregnancy is usually fine, but carriers should be consulted as regulations for individual carriers may vary.

The Religious Traveler

Many airline are able to cater for most meal requirements. All specific meal requests are described as "special meals" regardless of whether the request is based on religious belief, health or dietary considerations.

Over to you

1. What are the special requests and needs that passengers have? As an agent, how do you assist your passengers to solve their difficulties?
2. One of your passengers is inquiring about baby service. Tell her what you've known, such as age, fare, seat occupation and in-flight baby service.

★ Further Reading 2

Children traveling unaccompanied

Unaccompanied minor service is offered for children of 5~17 years of age. The service is mandatory for unaccompanied minors of 5~11 years old and optional for those of 12~17 years old. If the child is traveling as an unaccompanied minor, he or she may not travel on the last direct or connecting flight of the day. Be aware that the responsible adult bringing the child to the airport (including camp counselors, etc.) must remain at the airport until the child boards and the aircraft departs the gate.

Children aged 5 through 11 may travel alone as unaccompanied minors. Children aged 5~7 may travel on flights that are nonstop or do not require a change of airplane. They may not travel on connecting flights. They may also travel on the last nonstop flight of the day. Children aged 8~11 may travel on flights that are nonstop, direct and connecting flights (A direct flight makes a stop but there is no plane change.). They may also travel unaccompanied on connecting flights to other airlines. Children aged 8~11 are restricted from connecting to the last flight of the day which includes the last direct flight of the day. An exception can be made for children connecting to and from international flights. For children aged 12~17 years, the unaccompanied minor service is available, but not required, for this age group standard fees will apply.

When two or more unaccompanied minor are traveling together, the most restrictive age requirements will apply. For example, an 11-year-old child traveling with a 6-year-old may only travel on nonstop flights or flights that do not require a change of airplane.

The responsible adult may wonder how you will keep track of their child. An unaccompanied minor form must first be completed. During travel, children are given a bright red-and-white striped button to pin on their clothes. This button easily identifies unaccompanied children to our staff on the ground and in the air.

Over to you

1. Children of what age can be offered unaccompanied minor service?
2. How will the unaccompanied children be kept track?

Unit 7

Flight Irregularity

✥ *Discussion*

In airline service there are many factors which will affect the departure and arrival of the flights. Some may even cause the cancellation of the flight. Can you list some of the factors that may cause the delay and the cancellation of the flights?

✥ *Dialogue—A Delayed Flight* 延误航班

Announcement:
Passengers for Paris, may I have your attention, please? Flight AF679 for Paris will be delayed for an hour. Passengers for Paris, please wait in the terminal building. We will announce again when we get further information. Thank you.

P: We'll have to wait here for an hour. Excuse me. I can see our plane parking there. Is there any mechanical trouble with the plane?

C: No, it is owing to the thunderstorm at Guangzhou airport.

P: Maybe the rain will stop when we get there. So I think we should have a try.

C: The weather forecast says it won't stop raining within 2 hours. We cannot fly below the weather standards in order to ensure the safety of our passengers and the aircraft.

P: You do put the safety at the first place.

Unit 7 Flight Irregularity

C: This is our policy for service. Be patient, please.

VOCABULARY ASSISTANT

terminal 航班的   mechanical 机械的
owing to 由于   standard 标准

Complete the following dialogue.

C: Good morning, Sir. 1_____? (有什么为您效劳的吗?)

P: Good morning, I have been waiting for the departure of my flight for one and a half hours. Why isn't Flight SZ405 ready for boarding yet?

C: 2_____. (班机延误了。)

P: Do you know the reasons for the delay?

C: 3_____. (由于今天早上能见度很低。)

P: When do you expect it to depart?

C: 4_____. (大约2小时后。)

P: That's a long delay. That means I have to leave after lunch.

C: We like to offer you lunch free of charge in the airport restaurant. Please present the coucher to the waiter there.

P: How can I get the restaurant?

C: 5_____. (在地下一层。)

P: Thank you!

C: It's my pleasure.

If the flight has been delayed or cancelled what will you do for your passenger? Here are some pictures which may help you, could you think of other services?

entertainment   accommodation   food   beverage

Fill in the blanks with words given below. Change the form when necessary.

| endorse | regret | delayed | change | inform |
| put | response | apologize | supplying | |

1. I _____ to tell you that the flight has been cancelled.
2. The flight is _____ because of poor visibility.
3. We are sorry to _____ you that the flight will be delayed for 3 hours due to a thunderstorm.
4. We are now _____ beverages free of charge for delayed passengers.
5. We would like to _____ for the inconvenience caused by this delay.
6. We will be _____ for your meals and accommodation.
7. I'll try and see if I could _____ you on another flight.
8. I'll _____ your ticket to Air China and _____ the reservation details on your ticket.

Dialogue—Offering Special Service to Delayed Passengers 为延误乘客提供服务

Setting: Flight CA959 to Bangkok is delayed because of a thunderstorm on route. Cindy is offering special service to a delayed passenger.

> Announcement:
> Attention please. Passengers for Bangkok by flight CA595, I regret to inform you that this flight will be delayed for 3 hours due to a thunderstorm on route. Please go to waiting room 12 on the ground floor.

Cindy: Mr. Chen. I'm very sorry to inform you that your flight today has been delayed due to a thunderstorm on route.

Passenger 1: What's the extent of the delay?

Cindy: About three hours. The new estimated time of departure will be 12:30 p.m.

Passenger 1: That's a long delay. I have to leave after lunch time.

Cindy: We are sorry about the delay. We would like to offer you lunch in any restaurant in the airport. Please just present this voucher to the waiter. Enjoy your meal, Mr. Chen.

Passenger 2: Where is waiting room number 12?

Cindy: Go along the elevator, then go down the stairs and turn right. You will see a sign showing number 12 or you can follow me in a short while.

Unit 7 Flight Irregularity

At number 14 waiting room

Passenger 3: Where can I get something to drink?

Cindy: We are now supplying beverage free of charge for delayed passengers. Please show us your boarding pass.

Passenger 3: Thank you. Excuse me, do you have weiqi or chess here?

Cindy: Yes, we have.

Passenger 3: May I borrow a chess set?

Cindy: Yes. Please leave your boarding pass here. I'll give it back to you when you return the chess set.

> **Information Bank—缩写形式**
> **ETD:** estimated time of departure 预计起飞时间
> **ETA:** estimated time of arrival 预计到达时间
> **ATD:** actual time of departure 实际起飞时间
> **ATA:** actual time of arrival 实际到达时间

Passenger 4: Excuse me, where can I make a long-distance call?

Cindy: If you have an IC card, you can make the long-distance call over there. There are IC card telephones on the wall. Or you can go to the post office on the first floor on the west side of the terminal building.

Passenger 5: Where is the washroom?

> **VOCABULARY ASSISTANT**
> thunderstorm 雷暴   extent 限度、范围
> estimate 估计   voucher 凭单
> chess 象棋   long-distance call 长途电话

Cindy: On both sides of the terminal building.

Passenger 5: Thank you!

■ Rearrange the dialogue in the right order and practice with your partner.

a. Because the airport in Montreal has been closed due to bad weather conditions.

b. Arranging accommodation

c. When shall I know if I can leave today?

d. How long will the delay last?

e. Perhaps I have to stay here for the night. How do I arrange tonight's accommodation?

f. Thank you for your undertanding and cooperation.

g. Good afternoon.

h. We would like to apoloigize for the inconvenience caused by this delay.

i. That's a long delay.

j. Yes. It has been delayed.

k. Thank you for telling me all this.

l. Good afternoon. I wonder if my flight has been delayed.

m. Could you tell me why?

n. The last word will come out around seven o'clock this evening and you will be informed then.
o. Flight CZ373 to Montreal.
q. What's your flight number?
p. Don't worry. If you have to stay here for the night, we will be responsible for your meals and accommodation.
r. I'm sorry. It's not sure yet. Maybe two or three hours.

Pair Work

Please make apologies to the following passengers and offer proper services to them.

(1) The flight for Hong Kong is delayed due to engine trouble. At the waiting room, one passenger asked for something to read; another passenger asks for something to play.

(2) Because of the bad weather, the flight for Philadelphia is delayed. Proper beverages will be offered.

(3) It's lunch time but an unexpected thunderstorm holds up several outgoing flights in the afternoon. The passengers have to wait until the weather conditions improve.

Language Practice—Making Apologies

> I'm very sorry...
> I'm sorry we tried our best, but...
> We regret to say...
> I apologize for ...
> Please excuse me for...
> We know this is very frustrating and inconvenient for you, but...

Pair Work—Making Apologies

Model: Passenger is upset about the flight being delayed for three hours' maintenance.

We regret to tell you that your flight has been delayed. Due to aircraft maintenance the delay will last for about 3 hours.

1. Passenger's angry about not being allowed to board the flight because of overbooking.
2. Passenger's upset about the flight being cancelled due to the sudden change in schedule.
3. Passenger's unsatisfied with his flight being delayed due to a technical fault.

Language Practice—Providing Information About the Delayed Flights.

Model: Flight FM951 to Macau—delay of two hours—due to aircraft maintenance—ETD: 7 p.m. —drink available in the departure lounge

I'm sorry, Mr. Jim, that your flight FM951 to Macau will be delayed for two hours due to aircraft maintenance. The estimated time of departure is 7 p.m. Drink is offered to all the delayed passengers. It is available in the departure lounge on a complimentary basis.

1. CA951 to Tokyo—delay of 3 hours—due to aircraft rotation—ETD: 21:40 p.m. —drink service provided in the waiting lounge
2. MU505 for Singapore—delay of 5 hours—because of thunderstorm—ETD: 22:45 p.m.—drink service available in the waiting lounge

Practice the following announcement.

Announcement:

Passengers for Moscow, attention please. I am sorry to inform you that your flight FM386 is cancelled at last. And I am sorry to keep you wait for more than 2 hours. You cannot get to Moscow today owing to the heavy snow in Beijing and thick fog in Moscow. Since you'll have to stay in Beijing tonight, we will accommodate you with food and lodging free of charge. Those who need free accommodation please go to counter A1 to register. We have limousines to take you to the hotel in 20 minutes.

Dialogue—Rerouting Passengers 为乘客变更旅程

P: Hello, miss. Could you tell me why flight MU154 to Dublin has been delayed?

C: It has been delayed because of engine trouble.

P: When will it be ready for departure?

C: Not until tomorrow morning.

P: That's too bad. I must arrive in Dublin today or I will miss a very important appointment. Is there another flight available?

C: Well, I'll try and see if I can put you on another flight.

P: Thank you.

C: Yes. Flight CA342 leaves in an hour.

P: Could you get me on that flight?

C: I'll check to see if there's any space left. OK. There are still two seats left.

P: That's great.

C: I'll endorse your ticket to Air China and change the reservation details on your ticket.

P: Thank you very much for your help.

C: Glad to be of service. That's why we are here.

How do you handle the following situation?

1) Mr. Yao's flight MU505 to Seoul has been cancelled due to flight maintenance. Reroute the passenger with flight CA609 which leaves at 1:00 p.m. and arrives at 4:15 p.m.

2) Heavy snow has caused flight CA612 delayed. Miss Smith wants to change her flight to BA312 which leaves the day after tomorrow.

Dialogue—Flight Cancellation 取消航班

Announcement:
Passengers for Berlin, may I have your attention, please. I'm very sorry to inform you that your flight MU521 is cancelled because of mechanical problems. You are asked to go to counter F3 to change to the following flights of China Eastern Airlines. Thank you for your cooperation.

P: That's too bad for me. I have an important private business to do tonight so I have to get there before 5 o'clock this afternoon.
C: Don't worry. There are 4 flights left for today. You can choose one of them to get there in time.
P: Yes, I can. But my friend will meet me at the airport. I don't like to trouble him more.
C: So you'd better give him a call as soon as you select a new flight.
P: Good idea. Thank you very much.

Dialogue—Rerouting a Passenger Due to Flight Cancellation 由于航班取消而为乘客变更旅程

C: I'm afraid, Miss Yuan, that Flight MU613 to Vienna has been cancelled due to technical trouble. Our reservation section has been trying to contact you, but we were unable to reach you at the number you gave us.
P: I'm sorry I've been out for business trip last week and just came back. Then what are you going to do with my flight?
C: I can rebook you on the same flight tomorrow. Of course, we'll put you up free at the airport hotel tonight.
P: Isn't there any flight today? I must arrive there for an important international conference.
C: There is the Korean Airline flight 121 that leaves in 50 minutes and arrives at 6:00 p.m.
P: That's good. I'll take this flight.
C: Let me check the seats on the flight.

Unit 7 Flight Irregularity

➕ **Complete the following dialogue with the given words and practice with your partner.**

| arrangements | reservation | connect | change | maintenance |
| schedule | prefer | urgent | endorse | send |

C: Mr. Zhang, I see that you are going to Beijing to _____ with CA921 to Osaka. I'm very sorry your flight CA921 today has been cancelled for _____ reasons. I can either book you on the same flight tomorrow or I can make a _____ on the Japan Airlines flight 786 today which leaves Beijing at 3:10 p.m. and arrives in Osaka at 7:10 p.m. which would you _____, Mr. Zhang?

P: I must arrive in Osaka today due to my _____ business. So, I will take the Japan Airlines flight.

C: OK. I'll _____ your ticket to Japan Airlines and _____ the reservation details on your ticket.

...

C: Here is your ticket. Mr. Zhang, we can _____ a telex or fax to advise your party of your change in _____, or make a call courtesy of Air China. Which would you prefer?

P: I prefer to call my receiving party in Beijing asking for new _____ for me to be met at the airport.

➕ **Read the dialogue above carefully and give proper response to the following questions.**

1. Could you tell me why the flight CA403 has been delayed?
   _____

2. When will it be ready for departure?
   _____

3. Is there another flight available?
   _____

4. Could you get me on that flight?
   _____

🞢 Read these useful sentences and translate them into Chinese.

> I'll try and see if I could put you on another fight.
> I'll check to see if there's any space left.
> I'll endorse your ticket to Air China and change the reservation details on your ticket.
> Glad to be of service.

🞢 Try to use the following phrases to start handling upset passengers.

1. CA316 to Osaka—cancelled—typhoon—rebook a flight for tomorrow morning—offer accommodation and meals in the airport restaurant
2. MU515 for Moscow—cancelled—heavy snow—rebook a flight for tomorrow—meals and lodgings provided free in the airport hotel

🞢 Listen to the passage and fill in the blanks—Overbooking.

Overbooking is a term used to describe the sale of access to a service which exceeds the capacity of the service. 1_____ can book more customers onto a vehicle than can actually be accommodated by an aircraft, train, or cruise ship. This allows them to have a (nearly)

full vehicle on most runs, even if some customers 2_____ (tickets are often rebookable afterwards). 3_____ often cancel at the last minute, when their meetings take more time than planned. If everyone shows up, at least in the case of airlines, the overbooking will cause 4_____. Airlines may ask for volunteers to 5_____, and/or refuse boarding to certain passengers, in exchange for a compensation that may include an additional 6_____ in a later flight. They can do this and still make more money than if they booked only to the plane's capacity and had it take off with empty seats. Some airlines do not overbook as a policy that provides incentive and avoids customer disappointment. They have mostly tourists and their tickets are 7_____, so their passengers show up. A few airline frequent flyer programs actually allow a customer the privilege of flying an already overbooked flight; another customer will be asked to leave. Often only 8_____ is overbooked while higher classes are not, allowing the airline to upgrade some passengers to otherwise unused seats.

🞢 Over to you

1. What is overbooking?
2. Why do the airline companies overbook?

3. What will the airline companies do if the flight is overbooked?

Dialogue—Overbooking 机票超售

C: Mr. Zhou, I'm sorry but we are not able to board you on the plane today.

P: How come? I have a reserved ticket. Why should I not be allowed to board the plane. I'm very annoyed.

C: We know this is very frustrating and inconvenient for you but all the passengers have checked-in and already boarded the plane. There is not a single seat left on the plane.

P: I must leave today for a business talk.

C: Mr. Zhou, we are looking for someone who would be willing to give up his seat on the flight today in exchange for 2000 RMB and a confirmationed seat on tomorrow's flight.

P: I'll keep my fingers crossed.

...

C: Thank you very much for your patience. I'm sorry we tried our best but have not been able to find a passenger who will volunteer to give up his seat.

P: That's too bad.

C: There are several things we can do now. we can rebook you on our flight tomorrow and we would offer you accommodation, meals and a cheque for 2000 RMB in recognition of the inconvenience this causes you.

P: All right. Please rebook me, on a flight tomorrow morning.

C: We will. Thank you for your understanding and cooperation.

VOCABULARY ASSISTANT

annoy 使烦恼、使生气　　　frustrating 令人沮丧的
confirmationed 确定的　　　volunteer 自愿(做、提供)
recognition 承认　　　　　　cooperation 合作
keep my fingers crossed 但愿能够成功、祈祷能够成功

Information Bank

因超售等原因不能提供旅客预先订妥的座位,称拉客。拉客的程序一般是:
1. 无订座记录旅客
2. 本站始发的本公司工作人员
3. 原机过境的本公司工作人员
4. 免票旅客
5. 享受 50%以下优待折扣的其他空运企业人员家属
6. 经济舱旅客
7. 乘机航段最短或无联程航段的旅客
8. 中国籍旅客
9. 外国籍无急事和身份较低的旅客

★ Further Reading 1

Airline Delays and Cancellations

Complaints about airlines are increasing each year, but there is evidence that it's rare that consumers get compensation due to flight delays, though the depays may easily happen. In the UK, since February 2005, airlines, which unexpectedly cancel or delay a flight, must compensate customers. Passengers who are denied boarding are entitiles to a compensation of 250~600 Euro depending on the length of the flight.

In the event of a delay exceeding 3 hours, customers should receive light refreshments.

In the event of a delay exceeding 6 hours, customers should receive a main meal.

In the event of a longer delay, wherever possible, customers should receive meals and accommodation appropriate for the time of day.

In the event of a delay to a charter flight, the operator shall ensure that as early as possible there must be communication to customers of reasons for and the extent of any delays, together with an obligation to make appropriate welfare provisions.

However, some airlines are ignoring the regulations. When airlines delay or cancel a flight, they are obliged to tell consumers of their rights, but often don't. When a passenger demands compensation, some either hide behind get-out clauses or hope the customer will simply be tired of the process and give up.

If passengers are wrongly denied compensation, the small claims court is the best option. Until more passengers take this route, airlines will doubtlessly continues to cancel flights in the knowledge they will aviod most claims.

➕ *Over to you*

1. On what occasions can a passenger get compensation?
2. How much compensation can a passenger get if the flight is delayed for a day?
3. Why is it not easier for the passengers to get the compensation?
4. In what way can a passenger get the compensation due to flight delays?
5. Try to find some ways to ease the passengers' anxiety due to a long flight delay.

★ Further Reading 2

What Air Carriers Should Do For Delayed Passengers

Flight delays are an unavoidable part of air travel as airplanes operate in an enviornment that is fully exposed to the changeable weather, especially in winter, when weather-related delays are to be expected. Then too, while aircraft are dependable, mechanical parts can wear out and when they do, delays are nearly inevitable. When the breakdown occurs in some remote corner of the world, delays can stretch into days. The problem is not that there are delays. It is more "How do airlines deal with their passengers when faced with delays?"

Regardless of the seriousness of the delay, whether it is a few hours or a few days, airlines have the responsibility to keep passengers advised as to what is happening and when it is likely to be fixed. This is no easy task, particularly with creeping delays, but it is essential that travellers not be left in the dark when things go wrong. Most passengers will readily recognise and appreciate the effort. So, what should airlines do?

A. Provide food and drink

While in the case of relatively short delays, those under four hours, good communications can do much to relieve passengers' concerns and frustrations. However, much more needs to be done as delays begin to stretch beyond that point. When delays extend over normal mealtimes, all passengers, not just those who ask, should be provided with food and drink. If this is done by way of meal vouchers, then carriers should ensure that the value of the coupons is such that passengers can purchase a reasonable meal. Carriers should also ensure that there are outlets available where the coupons may be used.

B. Allow passengers to go back to the gate

When there is a significant delay and passengers have already boarded the aircraft, every effort should be made, consistent with safety and security, to return passengers to the terminal. This is especially important when an aircraft's heating or cooling systems are inoperative. Lengthy, on-aircraft delays under sweltering conditions with no food, drink or reliable information, are all too common.

C. Provide overnight accommodation

When delays extend into the "normal" sleeping hours from 11 p.m. to at least 6 a.m., it is not unreasonale to expect that sleeping accommodation be provided to passengers. If they are near their residence the transportation to and from home will be provided along with clear instructions about the time by which they are expected to be back at the departure gate. Passengers should also be provided with a means of advising people waiting for them at destination of the delay and their likely arrival time.

D. Allow delayed passengers to cancel their trip

Most serious of all are those delays that extend beyond eight hours. In such cases, when the delay happens at the point of origin, passengers should be provided with the opportunity to cancel their trips and to receive a full refund, even if their tickets are of the non-refundable type.

E. Offer tangible compensation

If passengers take alternative travel because of more than eight-hour delay, they should be offered a cash refund of a significant portion of the airfare they paid. In addition, passengers could be awarded bonus frequent flyer points or vouchers for future travel.

F. Offer transportation on another airline

Passengers should be offered alternate travel arrangements at the carrier's expense. Carriers should make arrangements to have their delayed passengers transported on the available flight, whether on their own airline or on another carrier.

G. Included irregular operations procedures in the tariff

Carriers' policies in regards to compensation and customer care during delays should be included in their tariffs and clearly displayed at check-in and boarding gates, where practicable.

Over to you

1. What's the best way to relieve passengers' worries and frustrations when the delays extend over normal mealtimes?
2. In which case, according to the writer, should passengers be allowed to cancel their trip and receive a full refund?
3. Do you think that carriers should be responsible for offering alternate travel arrangements to their delayed passengers?

Unit 8

Other Services

Part I Lost and Found
失物招领

■ *Have you lost something? You have left an article at the airport?*

■ *Dialogue—Lost and Found（1）失物招领*

P: Hello! Is this Lost and Found?

C: Yes. What can I do for you?

P: I'd like to know if someone has picked up a laptop computer that I lost on flight CA621 this morning.

C: What type is it?

P: Lenovo 3000.

C: Would you show me your passport?

P: Here is my passport, miss.

C: Would you please wait here for a moment?
   Let me have a look on the shelf. I'm sorry, sir.
   There isn't your laptop computer. Did you say you lost it on flight CA621 this morning?

P: Yes, I'm sure I lost it on that flight.

C: You see it is only 4 o'clock in the afternoon. China Airline is a very responsible company. I think if someone picked it up.

P: OK! I'll come here later.

...

At 5 o'clock in the afternoon

P: Hello, miss.

> **VOCABULARY ASSISTANT**
>
> laptop computer 手提电脑
> shelf 架子   responsible 负责任的

C: Hello, sir. A laptop computer was sent here a moment ago. It looks like the one you described.

P: Is there my name on the bag?

C: Yes. It is the same as the one on your passport. Here you are, sir. Would you please sign your name on this form?

P: OK! Thank you very much. Good-bye!

Dialogue—Lost and Found (2) 失物招领

P: Excuse me. I lost my briefcase in the waiting hall this morning.

C: I'm sorry to hear that. We will try to find it for you. Would you please leave your name and telephone number in New York?

P: Yes. My name is Shang Nan and my telephone number is (212) 5321124.

C: Would you tell me something about your briefcase in detail?

P: Certainly. It is black, about 30 cm tall, 20 cm long, and 10 cm wide.

C: What's in it then?

P: Well, my passport, 4 traveler's checks, some business documents, 1,000 dollars in cash.

C: Anything else?

P: Well, there are some other things, but I cannot name them at the moment.

C: OK! If anyone sends back here a briefcase like yours, we would inform you to come to check it. I think it's better for you to ring us up. The number is (202)4561122.

P: OK! I would. Bye-bye!

Two days later

P: Hello! This is Shang Nan speaking.

C: Hello! This is Lost and Found of Beijing Airport. What can I do for you, sir?

P: Two days ago I went to your office to see whether you got my briefcase.

C: Oh, I see. But so far we haven't got any briefcase like yours.

P: I'm so sorry to hear that. Should I phone you again?

C: Yes, two days later, please. Bye-bye!

Two more days later

P: Hello! This is Shang Nan speaking.

C: Hello! Mr. Shang. We have tried to locate your briefcase. But so far we haven't found it yet. We'll try again.

Unit 8 Other Services

P: I'm sorry to have troubled you so much.
C: Don't metion it.

Complete the following dialogue.

P: Excuse me, could you help me?
C: 1_____?
P: Well, I was wondering if anyone has turned in a passport.
C: 2_____?
P: I think so. I can't find it anywhere in my hotel room, and I remember I used it yesterday in this duty-free shop.
C: 3_____?
P: In the suit-dress department. I had to show it to pay for these dresses with my traveler's checks.
C: 4_____.
(a minute later)
P: 5_____.
C: Then what shall I do?
P: 6_____.
C: Do you have a pen?
P: Here you are.
C: Oh, I seem to lose things every time I travel.

> a. I'm afraid not. Have you lost your passport?
> b. Well, let me call the suit-dress department to see if they've found a passport.
> c. Sorry, your passport has not been found there, either.
> d. Yes. What's the problem?
> e. Where exactly did you use your passport in the shop?
> f. You can fill in this lost property report, and I'll keep my eyes on it.

Lost Property Report —A form the property owner has to fill in which describes lost items.

To report any item lost in the Airport Terminal, Parking Garage or drive areas, please fill out the form below as completely as possible.

Please note: If you navigate away from this page before you have completed and submitted it, any information you provided will be lost and you will have to begin the process again.

For items lost or left on an airplane, please contact your airline.

Date & Location Information:

Date Lost: 4/2/2018　4/2/2018

Location Lost: Airport Drive/Curbside

Location Details:

Contact Information:

*Name (First, Last):

Address:

City:

State: (none)

Zip/Postal Code:

Country: UNITED STATES

*Phone:　(not specified)

Alternate Phone:　(not specified)

Email:

Clear　Next

Unit 8 Other Services

Information Bank

Traveler's check: A type of check designed especially for business or vacation travelers. The traveler pays for the checks in advance. Thus the check is an order from the issuing company to pay on demand. Traveler's checks may be cashed almost anywhere in the world, and are insured against loss, theft, or destruction.

Make up your own dialogues between flight attendants and passengers using the following sentence patterns.

Clerk at the Lost and Found Office	Passengers
★ What's the matter? ★ I am sorry to hear that. ★ Could you please give me a detailed description? ★ What's in it? ★ ...it looks like the one you described just now. ★ That's nothing. Glad to be of assistance.	★ Is this the Lost and Found office? ★ I lost my ... in .... ★ It is..., and it contains... ★ Thank you ever so much for your help.

Dialogue 3—Lost and Found (3) 失物招领

Setting: A passenger has just lost his boarding card before going through security.

P: Excuse me, I'm terribly sorry, but I've lost my boarding card!

C: Oh, have you checked everywhere for it?

P: Yes, I have. I can't find it. What am I going to do?

C: Just take another few minutes and check all your pockets and your hand luggage! OK?

5 minutes later

P: No, I can't find it. I'm so sorry!

C: You shouldn't be so careless, sir.

P: I know. Will I have to buy another ticket?

C: No, no. Relax. I'll just print another boarding card for you.

P: Oh, thank you so much.

C: May I have your passport, please?

P: Yes, of course. Here you are.

C: Here is your boarding card. Your seat is in Row 11C and your boarding time is 1:30. You will be boarding at Gate C11.

P: Thanks again.

C: No problem. Just make sure you keep this one safe!

P: I will.

C: Enjoy your flight. Bye.

P: Bye.

Part II Inquring Services
询问服务

Listen and practice—Inquring about Flights 询问航班情况

C: Hello. Can I help you?

P: Yes, I plan a trip to New York next week. Are there any direct flights from Beijing to New York?

C: Wait a moment please. I will check the exact schedule for you. (a moment later) 1_____ is scheduled 2_____.

P: Are there any extra flights during the Olympic games?

C: Yes. Flight CA531 departs at 3_____.

P: What's the flying time between Beijing and New York?

C: 4_____.

P: How much is the ticket?

C: 5_____.

P: Return?

C: 6_____?

P: By the way, is that a Boeing 747 flight?

C: Yes. It's a Boeing 747~400.

P: That's all I want to know. Thank you!

C: You're welcome. 7_____.

Unit 8 Other Services

Listen and Practice—Inquiring about Traveler's Files 询问乘机所带证件

P: Good morning, Miss. This is my first time to travel by air. I don't know the procedures I have to go through before boardng.

C: The procedures you have to go through depend on whether you are 1_____ passenger.

P: Oh, I think I am an international passenger. I'll take flight MU559 to Madrid this evening.

C: Have you got 2_____ with you?

P: I think so. I have got my passport, and the ticket.

C: What about the 3_____ on your ticket? Would you please show me your ticket?

P: Yes, here you are.

C: Good, your reservation status is OK.

P: What does that mean?

C: That means you can 4_____ on that flight. If your reservation status is RQ, especially when you make a 5_____ you cannot get your seat on the flight. RQ means your reservation is only requested but not confirmed.

P: Oh, I see. Anything else?

C: Have you got 6_____?

P: Oh, yes. Here it is.

C: OK! Have you paid your 7_____?

P: What, airport fee?

C: Yes. 8_____ leaving from any airport within China should pay 9_____ for airport fee. You should pay it first. And then you can go through 10_____.

C: OK, I'll pay it first. Thanks a lot.

Listen and Practice—Inquiring about Boarding Formalities 询问乘机手续

P: Excuse me. This is my first time to travel by air. There are so many people standing in lines. I feel very confused. I don't know which line I should stand in.

C: 1_____?

P: Yes. Here you are.

C: Are you going to 2_____?

P: International flight.

C: 3_____?

P: I'm going to New York.

C: Have you got your passport with 4_____?

P: Yes, here they are. Can you deal with all the formalities for me?

C: No, I can't. I just want to know whether they are ready. You have to 5_____.

P: I see.

C: OK! All your travel documents are ready. Now, please go there and 6_____ first, and then go into 7_____ to check in for your flight, and 8_____. After this, you'll get 9_____. Then you should follow other passengers to go through 10_____. When it's time to board the plane, you may board your flight.

P: Thank you for your help.

✈ Listen and Practice—Inquiring about Flight Connection 询问转机

C: 1_____?

P: Oh, yes. My flight just landed at 6:50 a.m. and my KLM flight leaves at 8:40 a.m. I was wondering if this is enough time to get my bags from my flight to Boston and to hop on the flight to AMS? If there isn't enough time, I'll have to cancel my next flight.

C: You have nearly 2 hours, and you may need it. It's a big airport for sure. Let me show you. If you are changing airlines you'll probably need to 2_____, then 3_____, then get to 4_____ to the flight to AMS, then go through 5_____.

P: Oh, my god! I'm not sure whether I'll have to change airlines. Can you help me check?

C: Of course, sir. Yes, they are different airlines. But, let me see...Luckily, sir, you don't have to change airline because they are partner airlines.

P: You mean...?

C: Things are getting easier now. Your bags should go straight through and you should not have to clear customs.

P: Take your time, sir, and enjoy your stay at the airport.

✈ Listen and Practice—Inquiring about Arrival Time 询问航班到港情况

P: Good moring, miss. Can you tell me the arrival time of flight XW102 from Kunming, please? The scheduled time of arrival of XW102 is 17:20, but it's already 18:00.

C: Yes. 1_____ will be 2_____. The weather in Changsha is not good. 3_____.

P: That's too bad. We have a delegation on that flight. And our cars have been waiting outside the termial building for half an hour.

C: I am sorry that your cars have to wait for about 1 more hour.

P: By the way, can you tell me the departure time of CA906 at Kunming? We have another delegation

Unit 8 Other Services

on that flight.

C: Well, its estimated time of departure is 4_____, but I don't know its actual time of departure. I have to ask 5_____. Would you please wait a moment?

...

OK! Its actual time of departure is 6_____.

P: Many thanks for your help.

Listen and Practice—Inquring about Flight Delay 询问晚点飞机情况

P: Excuse me, miss.

C: What can I do for you?

P: I've just heard an announcement that my flight has been delayed.

C: 1_____?

P: Flight MU530 to Seattle.

C: Yes, it's true. It has been delayed.

P: Could you please tell me why?

C: Yes, of course. The delay is 2_____.

P: How long will the delay be? Do you have any further information about it?

C: I am sorry, we don't know 3_____ at present. But according to 4_____, there will be a change in the weather soon.

P: We have to wait. Well, is it possible for the rain to stop before noon?

C: It's hard to say. Weather is so changeable in the summer. Please 5_____.

P: Yes, I will. Thanks a lot. Bye!

C: Bye!

Listen and Practice—Inquring about Charter Flight 询问包机

C: Hello. Can I help you?

P: Yes, I'm the leader of the French football team. We have already finished our match. We would like to charter a flight to go back to Paris.

C: 1_____?

P: We have 50 people, including the coaches and players together with some sportswear and sports equipment.

C: 2_____?

P: Next Tuesday.

C: It's Friday today. There are only 3 days left. I think 3_____ at such short notice. During the Olympic Games, there are many charter flights. You had better 4_____. But you can

119

have a try.

P: I think so. Where can I charter a flight?

C: You should go to Air China Booking Office to 5_____.

P: Where is the Air China Booking Office?

C: On the second floor of the terminal building, east side.

P: Thank you for your help.

C: You're welcome.

■ Listen and Practice—Inquiring about the Arrival Flight 询问航班到港情况

P: Will you please tell me where to go to meet flight MU548 from Bangkok arriving at 7:50 p.m.?

C: Well, 1_____ after the flight has landed the passengers will be coming through the 2_____ having 3_____.

P: About 30 minutes?

C: Yes. 4_____ on the first floor.

P: Thank you very much.

C: 5_____.

■ Read the above dialogues again and make a similar one according to the following situations.

1. Li Fang is going to meet her friend from Austria. She goes to the Information Desk to ask when the flight will arrive.
2. Mr. James wants to travel around China. He inquires about the flights to Zhangjiajie at the Information Desk.
3. Alan is going to take flight MU520 to Seoul. The flight should depart at 13:15. It's already 13:30, but they still haven't heard any boarding announcement. Therefore, they go to the Airport Information Desk to ask the reason for the delay and the extent of the delay.
4. Jeanine's flight to travel to Yunnan Province departs at 11:00 a.m. They go to the check-in counter to inquire about check-in time and procedures.

Part III   Flight Connection
转机服务

Unit 8 Other Services

✦ Dialogue—Flight Connection 转机

Passengers from San Francisco, you have arrived at Chicago Airport. Please proceed to the baggage claim area to get your baggage. Passengers who are going to fly on to other places go through the connection formalities and stay in the waiting hall. Please pay attention to the information about your flights.

P: Good morning, miss, I just came from New York and I'll fly to Washington today.

C: Have you made a reservation for the flight to Washington?

P: Yes, I have.

C: Which flight are you going to take?

P: Flight AA165, departing at 19:50.

C: Would you please show me your ticket?

P: Yes. Here it is.

C: Oh, good. Your reservation is OK. It is in order now.

P: It is only 15:40. There are more than 4 hours to go. May I go shopping now?

C: Of course you can. But you should remember to go to the check-in counter for the connection procedure no later than 19:00.

P: I would keep it in my mind. Thank you very much.

(Back to the check-in counter)

P: Excuse me, miss. This is my ticket for flight AA165.

C: Your ticket is OK. Your seat will be C4. Good-bye!

✦ Listen and Practice—Inquring about Flight Connection 询问转机

P: Excuse me.

C: Yes, sir. Can I help you?

P: I've just arrived from San Francisco and I'm going to fly to Qingdao to watch the Olympic canoeing contest. How can I make my connection?

C: 1_____?

P: Yes, I have. MU433.

C: 2_____?

P: Here is my ticket.

C: You should 3_____ at the Domestic Transfer Booking Office.

P: Where is the Domestic Transfer Booking Office?

C: On the second floor, east side.

P: By the way, so I have to claim and transfer my baggage?

121

C: Yes, 4_____.

P: I see. Sorry to have given you so much trouble.

C: 5_____.

Part IV Passenger Enquiries 乘机旅客查询

Listen and Practice—Passenger Enquiries 乘机旅客查询

Setting: At China Eastern Airline Information Desk Shanghai Hongqiao Airport

P: Would you please tell me if Mr. Wang Qiang is arriving on your flight from Madried today?

C: I'll be glad to check that for you. 1_____?

P: W-A-N-G Q-I-A-N-G

C: 2_____.

...

C: I show a Wang Qiang on the 3_____ for MU552, which will arrive in Shanghai at 4_____ this afternoon.

P: Flight MU552 and it gets in at 4:35 p.m. Thank you.

C: 5_____.

Dialogue—Passenger Enquiries (1) 乘机旅客查询

P: My friend is scheduled to come from London on your flight tomorrow. Could you please check if he is on your passenger namelist?

C: I'm afraid we haven't received the passenger namelist yet for our flight MU582. Would you mind calling again after 12:00 this afternoon? We won't have it until the flight departs.

P: But may I know if he has a reservation there?

C: Certainly. May I have his full name, please?

P: Yes, CHEN MING.

C: Thank you. Just a second and I'll check.

...

C: We are holding a reservation for Mr. Chen Ming on our flight MU582. The flight is scheduled to arrive in Beijing at 6:25 tomorrow morning. If you call us again this afternoon, we will tell you if he is definitely arriving on that flight. We also have actual arrival time for you at that time.

P: Thank you for your information.

C: You are welcome.

VOCABULARY ASSISTANT

schedule 安排   definitely 确切地

Unit 8 Other Services

Dialogue—Passenger Enquiries (2) 乘机旅客查询

P: I want to know if Miss Carol Smith is on your flight MU524 which gets in from Tokyo today.

C: I'll check the passenger namelist for you.

...

C: I'm afraid I don't show a Miss Carol Smith on the passenger namelist.

P: Is there any way to check if she will come in tomorrow?

C: Let me pull out her reservation record.

...

C: According to her reservation record, she has changed her reservation to MU524 tomorrow. It leaves Tokyo at 1:50 p.m. and arrives in Beijing at 3:50 p.m.

P: Really? She did not tell me about the change.

C: If you call after 2:00 tomorrow afternoon, we'll tell if she is definitely taking that flight.

P: Thank you very much.

C: You are welcome.

Part V Carry Service 行李搬运服务

Dialogue—Carry Service 行李搬运服务

C: Hello, sir. What can I do for you?

P: Yes. My boxes are too heavy to carry.

C: No problem. Please leave them to me. We offer the best baggage service. How many boxes do you want to be carried?

P: I'd like all these.

C: Let me count them first. Oh, seven boxes. They must give you a lot of trouble during your journey.

P: Yes. They are very heavy though not big. How much?

C: 3 yuan for each. 21 yuan in all.

P: Need I pay in advance?

C: No. Pay me when we arrive.

Part VI Airport Announcements
机场广播

Read the following announcements and then translate into Chinese.

Check-in

Good morning, ladies and gentlemen:
Air China flight CA861 to New York is now ready for check-in. Passengers on that flight please have your baggage and the tickets ready and proceed to the Air China counter 2. Thank you.

Check-in closing

Check-in for Air China flight CA452 bound to Wolverhampton will be closing in a few munites. Passengers who have not yet checked in please come to the Air China counter. Thank you.

Boarding Announcement for Delayed Departure

Thank you for waiting, ladies and gentlemen. The maintenance of the aircraft has been completed. Air China Flight 856 to San Francisco is now ready for boarding through Gate 5. Thank you.

Boarding

Attention please:
China Eastern Airline announces the departure of flight MU312 to Hong Kong. Passengers for this flight please proceed to Gate 4. Thank you.

Refreshments are Offered Due to Delay

Attention please. Air China Flight CA716 to Hong Kong will be delayed because of weather conditions at Hong Kong International Airport. A further announcement will be made not later than 10:00. In the meantime passengers are invited to take light refreshments with the compliments of the airlines at the buffet in this lounge.

Final Boarding Call

Attention please. This is the final call for passengers traveling to New York. Flight CA402 is now boarding. Passengers are kindly requested to proceed to Gate 13.

Delay Due to Miantenance

Your attention please. Air France regrets to announce that the departure of Flight AF907 to Paris will be delayed due to maintenance of the aircraft. New departure time will be announced at about 1:00. Passengers are requested to wait in this lounge until further notice. Thank you!

Irregularity Depay Due to Weather Definite Departure Time

May I have your attention please. China Eastern Airines regrets to announce that the departure of Flight MU123 to Qingdao will be delayed due to unfavorable weather conditions there. The new deparutre time will be 11:30. We expect to begin boarding at about 11:00 o'clock. Thank you!

Irregularity Depay Due to Weather Indefinite Time

May I have your attention please. Air China regrets to announce that the departure of Flight CA567 to Singapore will be delayed due to unfavorable weather conditions in Singapore. We are monitoring weather reports and will keep you informed. You are requested to wait in this lounge until further notice. Thank you!

Cancellations

Attention please. Air China Flight CA512 to Zurich has been cancelled because of weather conditions at local airport in London. Will passengers please collect their hand baggage and go to the rear exit of this lounge. Please have your passports ready and proceed downstairs to counter 17 where information about re-bookings, refunds and alternative transport is available.

Paging for Claiming Baggage

China Eastern Airlines paging Miss Carol arriving on Flight CA312 for Los Angeles. Will Miss Carol please come to the information counter in the baggage claim area. Thank you.

Paging Arrival

Attention please. Japan Airlines Flight 412 for Tokyo. Now arriving at Gate 14.

Paging for Standby Passenger

Attention please. Standby passengers for China Eastern Airlines Flight MU1432 to Guangzhou please come to the counter 13. Thank you.

★ Further Reading

Flight Transfer 转机

Passengers who already have boarding passes for their next flight may proceed directly to the departure gate, no matter whether they arrive from a domestic flight or an international flight.

Passengers arriving from international flights with an immediate domestic connecting flight and who already have boarding passes for their next flight will have to clear Custom Immigration Quarantine (CIQ) before proceeding to the departure gate. Those without boarding passes should proceed to the transfer counters and check in before going to the departure gate.

In some cases transit passengers will need to pick up their baggage, even though they are continuing their journey on another flight. For instance, if they are traveling on another airline, they may need to collect their baggage first then check in for their next flight. Transit passengers do not need to collect their baggage when it has been labeled through to their destination and they have been given a boarding card for the next flight.

Transit passengers are also allowed to have a short visit outside of the airport while waiting for the connecting flight. This is applicable if transit time is more than 6 hours and upon approval by the Immigration Department. While away from the airport, transit passengers need to keep the correct documentation with them in case of any trouble. If they choose to leave the airport between flights, they must return no later than two hours before the flight departs. If a transit passenger is late for his flight, it will depart without him. His baggage will be off-loaded and he will not be allowed to travel.

Over to you

1. Where must international flight passengers requiring a domestic connecting flight go before proceeding to the departure gate?
2. Why are some transit passengers not required to collect their luggage?
3. Under what conditions are transit passengers allowed to leave the airport before their connecting flight?
4. What will happen if a connecting flight passenger is late for his flight?

Unit 9

Arrival Passengers' Formalities

◆ *Look at the formalities of departing or arriving for domestic or international passengers at the airport below, and could you add any and put them into right order?*

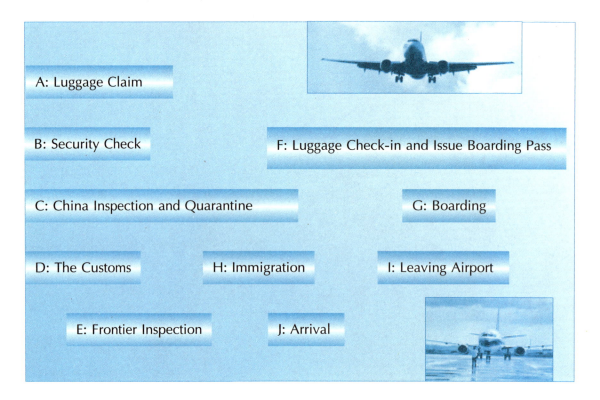

A: Luggage Claim

B: Security Check

F: Luggage Check-in and Issue Boarding Pass

C: China Inspection and Quarantine

G: Boarding

D: The Customs

H: Immigration

I: Leaving Airport

E: Frontier Inspection

J: Arrival

Unit 9 Arrival Passengers' Formalities

➕ *Discuss the following questions in pairs or in small groups and tell your partner what you will do in these situations.*

> What will you do if you find your luggage is missing?

> What vehicles do you prefer to take for transferring to the city center from the airport terminal?

> Have you ever experienced a delayed flight? What would you do if your connecting flight were delayed?

> How can you find a hotel in a city you've never been to?

➕ **Domestic Passengers** 国内旅客

Setting: Mr. Wang and his team which consists of 9 team members have been to Shanghai on business for one week. Now they are landing at Beijing Airport on CA 157.

➕ *Step 1   Arrival*

Dear Passengers, if the airplane stops at boarding bridge of the Terminal Building, you can enter the Luggage Claim Hall on the 1st floor along the airport passage of the 3rd floor; if you arrive at the Terminal Building by ferry bus, you can enter the Luggage Claim Hall directly after getting off the bus.

➕ *Step 2   Luggage Claim*

Luggage Claim Hall is located on the 1st floor, with Luggage Claim Carousel Screen installed at its entrance. You can find out which carousel your luggage will be arriving from the screen.
If you have a lot of luggage, you can use luggage trolley for free or choose trolley service.
In order to prevent your luggage from being mistakenly taken, airport personnel will check your luggage tag/number at the entrance. Your cooperation is highly appreciated.

Dialogue—Domestic Passengers（1）国内旅客

Read the following dialogues with your partner and finish the exercise below.

Setting: Mr. Wang and his team are going to the Luggage Claim Area.

C: Sir, what can I do for you?

P: We deplaned from flight MU268 just now. But now we don't know where to get my baggage.

C: You may go through this gate, and then you will be in the luggage claim hall for the domestic flights. Your baggage will be put on conveyer belt 3 in 5 minutes.

P: Thank you very much.

Dialogue—Domestic Passengers（2）Claiming Baggage 国内旅客认领行李

P1: Look! Our flight number has appeared on the screen.

P2: Yeah, the belt is moving. Our baggages will appear on the belt at once.

P1: I think you'd better stay behind to gather our suitcases. Let me take them down from the belt by myself.

P2: Let me help you. That will be too much for you.

P1: No problem. Look, my suitcase is coming.

P2: Mine is immediately after yours.

...

P1: Has everyone got your baggage?

P2: Yes, I've got mine. They all have got theirs.

P1: Good. Please wait here for a minute. I'm going to get some carts. Liu, could you please go with me?

P2: All right.

Dialogue—Domestic Passengers（2）Claiming Delayed Baggage 国内旅客认领行李

C: Sir, what can I do for you?

P: I've been waiting here for half an hour. All passengers coming with me have got theirs. I think they may have already left the airport by now. But I haven't got mine yet!

C: Would you please patiently wait for another 10 or 15 minutes?

P: I have to.

(Half an hour later)

P: Sorry, sir. I don't think my baggage can come today. What shall I do?

C: Could you please show me your baggage stubs?

P: Yes, here they are.

C: OK, I'll go to the airport inquiry office to have a check. Please wait.

(10 minutes later)

C: Sir, just now I went to the airport inquiry office. They called Shanghai Hongqiao International Airport.

Unit 9 Arrival Passengers' Formalities

P: What did they say?

C: A porter put your baggage in a wrong place; and your bags weren't loaded in the airplane you flew. But later on, they found the problem, and put them on the next flight.

P: When does the flight arrive here?

C: The interval between the two flights is only 1 hour. Since your flight arrived here about 50 minutes ago, it will arrive here in 30 minutes. Would you please go to the waiting room and have a short rest? When the flight arrives, I'll come here and help you claim your baggage.

P: OK! Thanks a lot.

(40 minutes later)

P: I've seen my baggage. Thank you for your help.

C: You're welcome.

Match the explanations with the words below.

1. luggage tag
2. shuttle bus
3. trunk
4. partner airlines
5. backpack
6. carousel
7. souvenir
8. Sheraton
9. circuit

a. A product purchased by a tourist as a reminder of a holiday.

b. The part of the bus that carries goods. Also known as the boot.

c. A large mechanical apparatus that carried luggage to air-travelers inside the airport.

d. A bag that is supported by the shoulders with double handles and lies across the back. Backpacks are supported on either one or both shoulders.

e. A label made of cardboard or plastic or metal attached to the luggage to show the identity of the luggage.

f. A bus serving as a transporting vehicle sending passengers from the airport to different places of the city.

g. The Sheraton hotel chain is a member of Starwood Hotels.

h. A journey or route all the way around a particular place or area.

i. Those could help you as passenger capture the award seat or earn miles faster toward a future free trip. As airlines have different partners with different regional networks, certain carriers may be more beneficial than others.

Step 3 Leaving Airport

You will enter the Greeting Hall after luggage claim, where you can meet your relatives and friends, ask for more information at Hotel Reception and Inquiry counter, or exchange currency at bank. Walking out for the Greeting Hall, you can choose airport bus or taxi to leave the airport.

Dialogue—Domestic Passengers (3) 国内旅客

Listen to the dialogue and fill out the blanks.

Setting: Mr. Wang and his team are going to the shuttle bus counter at the airport.

C: What can I do for you, sir?

P: I want to 1_____. Do you go there?

C: Yes, we have a bus leaving in 10 minutes. 2_____.
   The Jianguomen Hotel is the 4th stop. It takes about an hour.

P: That sounds good. We have a lot of luggage. Could you manage that?

C: Sure. The bus has a 3_____.

P: How much does it cost?

C: It's RMB 30. That's much cheaper than a taxi. But 4_____.

P: I'm happy with that. Thanks.

C: OK, please wait in 5_____ and the driver will call you when the bus is ready to leave. I hope 6_____.

Information Bank

I According to Notice on Inspection and Quarantine for Immigration to China, the following items are prohibited for entry:

Human's blood and its products;

Fruits, capsicum, eggplant and tomato;

Animal corpse and its specimen Soil;

Animal pathogen, destructive insect and other harmful organism;

Alive animal (except pet dog or cat) and animal's genetic material, including semen, fertilized egg and embryo, etc.;

Egg, pelt, bristle, coffin bone, horn, meat (including viscera) and their products; fresh milk, cheese, butter, cream, whey mist, silkworm chrysalis, silkworm egg, animal's blood and their products; aquatic animal products;

Transgenic biological material;

Worn-out clothes.

II According to applicable provisions issued by China Customs, the following items are prohibited for entry:

All kinds of weapons, imitative weapons, ammunition and explosive objects;

Spurious currency and feigned marketable securities;

Unit 9 Arrival Passengers' Formalities

Print, film, photo, disk, movie, tape, videotape, videodisc, laser disk, computer storage medium and other objects, which are harmful to Chinese politics, economy, culture and morality;

Various acrid poison;

Opium, morphine, diamorphine, bhang, as well as other dope and psychoactive drug that may cause addiction;

Animal, plant and their products, with dangerous germ, destructive insect and other harmful organism;

Food stuff, medicine or other objects, which are from epidemic areas and harmful to human and animal's health, or other pestiferous ones.

International Arrival

Setting: Mr. Williams and his family are landing at Beijing International Airport for sightseeing in China.

Step 1 Arrival

Read the statement below and get familiar with the formalities.

Good afternoon ladies and gentlemen. Welcome to Shanghai. Since 4 international flights have arrived at the airport almost at the same time, there are about 830 incoming passengers in the waiting hall. To shorten your delay at the airport and help you go through all the arrival procedures easily, we have assigned many clerks at all the counters. In order to go through the procedures as quickly as possible, please stand in queues and wait before the counters. Thank you.

VOCABULARY ASSISTANT

shorten 缩短   delay 耽搁、迟滞

Step 2 Inspection and Quarantine

According to the requirement of inspection and quarantine authorities, passengers are required to fill out Entry Health Quarantine Declaration Card honestly. Passengers from epidemic-stricken area of yellow fever should present valid vaccination certificate of yellow fever to Inspection and Quarantine authorities.

Step 3   Immigration

Overseas passengers should possess valid passport and entry visa; Chinese passengers should possess valid passport. On arrival of a Chinese port, passengers should present filled-in Entry Registration Card, together with passport and visa to the immigration check post for inspection.

Step 4   Baggage Claim

Dialogue—International Arrival Baggage Claim（1）Misloaded Baggage 国际旅客提取行李

Read the following situational dialogues and finish the exercises below.

P: Hello, Miss. I can't find my baggage here.

C: Don't worry, sir. Have you got your baggage check?

P: Yes, here you are.

C: Did you fly flight CA561 from New York?

P: Yes. I got here a moment ago.

C: Did you come here alone or with other people?

P: I came here with my family, my wife and my son. They've got theirs. I have two pieces, but so far I haven't got any.

C: All right. I'll try to help you find it. Maybe they will come on the next flight. How long will you stay here? And would you please leave your name, telephone number and address here?

P: OK. I'm Neal Williams. We'll sightsee here for 2 weeks. This is my address and telephone number in hotel.

C: If we get any information about it, I'll inform you, sir. And you may also call us up or come to the airport at any time. Sorry to have given you so much trouble.

P: No trouble at all. Bye.

（Three days later）

P: Hello. This is Neal Williams speaking.

C: Hello. This is Beijing International Airport. You are the gentleman looking for the lost baggage, aren't you?

P: Yes, I am.

> **VOCABULARY ASSISTANT**
>
> fax 传真
>
> Bangkok International Airport 曼谷国际机场

P: So far as I know, your baggage was not loaded on the flight you took. We have faxed New York Airport. They are trying to trace it. I'll tell you as soon as I get any information.

C: Well, thank you.

Unit 9 Arrival Passengers' Formalities

(Two more days later)

C: Hello, this is Beijing International Airport.

P: Hello, this is Neal.

C: Good news for you, Mr. Williams. Your baggage has been found in Bangkok International Airport. Do you want to have them sent here?

P: Yes, as soon as possible.

C: OK. I'll inform Bangkok International Airport of sending your baggage here as soon as possible.

P: Thank you again.

Answer the questions according to the dialogue above.

When you lose your baggage and inform the airport, what detailed information you need to offer to the clerk?

Dialogue—International Arrival Baggage Claim (2) Baggage Not Found
国际旅客提取行李

C: I'm sorry Mr. Williams; we're not able to locate your baggage yet.

P: What shall I do?

C: Please don't worry, sir. First we need to fill out a delayed baggage report and a customs clearance form. This will allow us to clear your baggage through customs on your behalf when your bag does arrive.

P: OK....Here you go.

C: You also need to complete an irregularity report. Make sure all the appropriate blanks are filled out.... Thank you. Sir, tracing efforts will begin immediately with our computerized tracing system. All bags that fit the description of the bag, both within Air China and all other major carriers worldwide, will be checked and then forwarded here on the first available flight.

P: You think my bag can be found?

C: It's hard to say, but our experience has shown that most missing bags arrive the next day.

P: OK, I'll call you to check tomorrow.

C: No, you needn't do that. We will contact you every day for the first four days and keep you apprised of the situation.

P: Fine. Thank you.

C: In the rare event that even after 96 hours we have been unable to locate your baggage, a

135

copy of your file will be forwarded to our Central Baggage Service Office in Beijing Air China. This department will then use its extensive tracing capabilities with all other carriers in an effort to locate your baggage. In any event, we will take full responsibility until the baggage is found or a fair compensation has been made.

P: But the thing is that I have no change of clothes and no daily necessities during my stay here.

C: Mr. Williams, we apologize for inconveniencing you in this way. We'd like to offer you up to RMB 200 to purchase any personal necessities you may need while waiting for your baggage to arrive.

P: Can I get cash from you?

C: According to our accounting regulations, you keep your receipt and send it to our office. We'll issue a check for the reimbursement. Mr. Williams, once again we apologize for this inconvenience and hope that this will not deter you from using Air China again in the future.

VOCABULARY ASSISTANT

locate 查找……的地点,定位　　customs clearance 结关,海关放行
irregularity 不规则,无规律　　trace 追踪　　apprise 通知
reimbursement 付还,退还　　deter 阻止

Dialogue—International Arrival Baggage Claim (3) Baggage Found 国际旅客提取行李

C: Good morning. Can I help you?

P: Yes. I'm afraid my suitcase is missing.

C: Don't worry. Could you tell me your flight number?

P: CA561 from New York.

C: Did you go to the right baggage claim area for your baggage?

P: Yes. I waited until all the bags came out on the conveyor belt.

C: May I see your ticket and baggage claim checks?

P: Here you are.

C: Sir, I see that you checked in 2 pieces of baggage. Did any of them come out?

P: Yes, only one piece and I did not find the other, my black suitcase.

C: Let me check unclaimed baggage records for you.

P: Thank you.

C: I'm sorry it's not in the records. I'll call our agent at the belt side to double check any left baggage.

P: ...What did they say?

C: I have a good news. We have located your suitcase, sir. It's lying by the belt side. Please follow me to belt No. 4 to pick up your suitcase.

P: Thank you very much.

C: You are welcome.

Dialogue—International Arrival Baggage Claim (4) Baggage Being Traced 国际旅客提取行李

Read the statement and the dialogue below, and do the situational role-play exercise with your partner.

Announcement

On our flights, more than 99% of checked luggage arrives on the same flight with the customer who checked the luggage. In the event your luggage does not arrive with your flight, we can assure you that everything possible will be done to locate your luggage and return it to you promptly.

If you are unable to locate checked luggage upon arrival, please go directly to our airline Luggage Service office located in airport.

Please Note: You must report any delayed luggage to us within 24 hours.

After you report your delayed luggage, we will immediately begin a search using the industry's automated luggage tracing system. You will be contacted when the luggage is located to schedule a delivery time and confirm your delivery address and information. You can also check for updates on the status of delayed luggage using our Luggage Tracking option or call the Luggage Information Line.

P: Excuse me. I've just arrived in Beijing from New York. Unfortunately my bags are missing. Would you please trace my bags?

C: Sure. What's your flight number, sir?

P: CA561 from New York.

C: Claim Hall 2 is for your flight. Did you go to the right claim area for your bags?

P: Yes, I waited until all the bags came out on the conveyor belt.

C: Where did you begin your journey, sir?

P: I started from New York and connected with CA in Tokyo.

C: Maybe, your bags were miscarried in Tokyo. May I have your baggage identification? I'll trace them right away. Please complete this questionnaire. It helps me a lot.

P: But the problem is that right now I don't have my necessary personal items with me.

C: We can cover up certain RMB worth of necessities for your temporary use.

P: OK. You'll expedite and deliver my baggage to my hotel, won't you?

C: Yes, we will. Please leave your hotel address and room number.

VOCABULARY ASSISTANT

track 跟踪   miscarry 被误送   expedite 加速

Make your own dialogue according to the situation given below.

The Olympic football player Mr. Baker has just arrived on Flight UN356. But his baggage is missing. He asks the clerk at the airport for help. The clerk helps him to find it at the baggage claim area.

Dialogue—International Arrival Baggage Claim (5) Baggage Damaged
国际旅客提取行李

Listen to the dialogues and fill out the blanks

P: Sir, my bag has just come out of the conveyor belt and I find 1_____.

C: I'm terribly sorry 2_____.

P: It was a new bag. I bought it not long before my departure.

C: Air China will 3_____ and return it to you within 3 days. In the unlikely event that 4_____, we will 5_____. Is that acceptable to you?

P: OK.

C: Would you please fill out 6_____?

P: OK... Here you are.

Unit 9 Arrival Passengers' Formalities

C: Thank you. 7_____. Once again, I would like to 8_____
_____.

◆ Dialogue—International Arrival Baggage Claim (6) Compensating for Lost Baggage 国际旅客提取行李

Put the dialogue into right order and read it with your partner to know as a clerk how to deal with a passenger who has lost his baggage.

Setting: After five days of tracing, Mr. Williams' lost bag has not been found. The Air China decides to pay compensation for his lost baggage.

Clerk

1. Yes, I do understand. We won't stop tracing your lost bag, though it's very difficult to say exactly how long it will take us to locate it. If it's located, we'll contact you immediately.
2. I'm sorry to say that despite extensive tracing, your baggage has not been found yet. Now we are prepared to pay you compensation for your loss according to the international regulations.
3. Hello, Mr. Williams.
4. Our maximum liability for international checked baggage is limited to RMB 60 per kilogram. Your lost baggage weighs 10 kilograms. Therefore, we'll pay RMB 600 as compensation fee.
5. Thank you for your cooperation. Please sign your name on this receipt for compensation.

Passenger

A. Hello, Miss. Have you found my lost bag?
B. Ok. I accept your payment.
C. Isn't it possible to locate my bag? You know, I just want to find my lost bag, not to get any compensation.
D. Well, how much will you pay for my lost baggage?

139

Step 5 The Customs

Read the statement and the dialogue below with your partner.

All inward/outward passengers, except those who are exempted from Customs inspection and control in accordance with relevant regulations or those under the age 16 who are traveling with accompanied adults, shall make a factual declaration to the Customs at airports of entry by completing a Declaration Form.

Passengers who select "No" in all the items on the Declaration Form may choose to go through "Nothing-to-declare Channel" ("Green Channel") for Customs procedures. Those who select "Yes" in the items on the Declaration Form shall provide in the corresponding spaces such details as description (type of currency), quantity (amount), model, etc., before choosing to go through "Goods-to-declare Channel" ("Red Channel").

Dialogue—At the Customs 机场海关

C: Welcome to China, Sir. Do you have anything to declare?

P: I don't think so. But I don't know what I should declare.

C: Have you got anything such as foods, fruits, vegetables and pets?

P: No, I carried none of them. And this is my health card.

C: So everything is OK. Thank you. Have a good stay here.

P: Thank you.

C: Do you have anything to declare, Miss?

P: I'm not sure about the fruits I've brought here.

C: Let me have a look. Hmm, I don't think you can take them into China.

P: What shall I do with them then?

C: Would you like to throw them await into that big bin over there?

P: But what if I would not like to?

C: Well, you'll have to pay RMB 500. But still you have to throw them away.

P: I will do as you said.

C: Thank you for your cooperation.

Step 6   Leaving Airport

You are going to enter the Greeting Hall, where you can meet your relatives and friends, ask for more information at Hotel Reception and Inquiry counter, or exchange currency at bank. Walking out for the Greeting Hall, you can choose airport bus or taxi to leave the airport.

Dialogue—Exchange Currency 兑换外汇

C: Good afternoon, sir. How can I help you?

P: I'd like to change some money.

C: OK. What kind of foreign currency have you got?

P: US dollars.

C: OK. Today's exchange rate is seven point one Yuan to one US dollar. How much would you like to change?

P: Four thousand US dollars. Please give me large bills.

C: No problem. Could you fill in this form?

P: Sure.... Is that all right?

C: Could you show me your passport?

P: Here you are.

C: Thank you. And I need your signature on the exchange form.

P: OK.

C: Thanks. Here's the money. Please check it.

P: Thank you very much.

Dialogue—Taking a Taxi 乘出租车

P: Miss, we've just arrived at the airport. Since this is our first time to come here, I don't know how to get the Friendship Hotel.

C: You have to take a taxi to get there. Although we have lots of limousines for passengers going downtown, none of them goes to the Friendship Hotel directly, 'cause you need to change a taxi or a bus to get the hotel then.

P: Oh, I see. Where can I get a taxi?

C: The Ground Transport Counter is over there. You can find a taxi there.

P: Thank you very much.

★ **Further Reading 1**

Charter Flight

A scheduled airline operates flights on a regular timetable between fixed points. A charter airline on the other hand, rents the entire plane and will fly it on any route at any time that is convenient to the passengers. With large modern planes, this would not be an efficient operation unless the group that was chartering or renting the plane was large enough to fill it. When a chartered plane carries a full load, it can offer much cheaper fares than a scheduled flight. On the main tourist routes, it is not difficult for enough people to get together to fill a large jet. The reduction of fares is the main selling advantage for charter flights.

In the passed few years, much traffic has gone to charter flights. The scheduled airlines have started to fight back in order to attract some of the customers back to them. They have also offered lower fares—youth fare—to special groups. The youth fare includes young people under 25 years of age. It is a special inducement to attract students, who make up a large part of the summer tourist traffic.

The airlines also offer package tours to their customers. A package tour includes not only the air fare, but also hotel accommodations, meals, sightseeing tours and any other "extras" to make the tour attractive. The air fare on the package tour is lower than the standard first-class or economy rate. Incidentally, several airlines also own hotels, so the package tours give them the additional benefit of assuring higher occupancy rates in their hotels.

At a large airline office, there is usually a special agent to handle all inquiries about charters. At smaller offices, a general sales representative makes the arrangements for chartering. In addition, the charter sales agent also offers individualized service. This might include reprints of special information about the group's destination. They might also include special food on the flight, special movies, special musical programs—in fact, anything that would make the trip more attractive to the chartering group. At the airport, at least one passenger through the check-in process; and the same service is provided at the destination.

The scheduled airlines have extended their interest to the charter business in recent years. Many of them have set aside several planes for chartering.

VOCABULARY ASSISTANT

efficient 有效的　　rent 租用　　inducement 引诱,动机
package 旅行社代办的旅游　　affinity 类似,亲近性

Over to you

1. Compared with scheduled flights, what advantage do charter flights have?
2. In order to get the run upon charter flights, what measures do scheduled airline take?

★ Further Reading 2

Northwest Airlines

Northwest Airlines began humbly on October 1, 1926 as a two-plane airmail carrier between Minneapolis/St. Paul and Chicago flying two rented open-cockpit biplanes.

From there, as the industry changed, several other airlines entered the Northwest family including: Republic Airlines, North Central Airlines, Southern Airways and Hughes Airwest. Current operating partners of Northwest, operating as Northwest Airlink are two regional airlines: Mesaba Airlines and Pinnacle Airlines.

Today, Northwest Airlines is the world's fourth largest airline with hubs at Detroit, Minneapolis/St. Paul, Memphis, Tokyo and Amsterdam and more than 1,700 daily departures. Northwest is a member of SkyTeam, an airline alliance that offers customers one of the world's most extensive global networks. With its affiliates, Northwest serves nearly 750 cities in almost 120 countries on six continents. Northwest employs 45,000 people worldwide with approximately 18,000 of them stationed in Minnesota.

Unit 10

Touring, Shopping and Entertaining in Airport

🔹 *Look at the following terms concerned with the services at the airport. Could you add any?*

- Control tower
- Runway
- Taxiway
- Apron
- Airlines
- Threshold
- Pier terminals
- Military Airport
- Maintenance area
- Hangar
- Freight
- Luggage
- Aircraft
- Satellite terminals
- Baggage handling
- Transporter terminals
- Commercial Airport
- General Aviation Airport
- Gate arrival terminals
- Duty-free store

Unit 10 Touring, Shopping and Entertaining in Airport

Now answer the questions

1. What are the three types of the airports? And what are the three types of the terminals?
2. What is a "duty-free store"?

VOCABULARY ASSISTANT

control tower 机场指挥塔台
runway 跑道
taxiway 滑行道
apron 停机坪
hangar 机库
threshold 跑道入口

Dialogue—Touring in the Airport (1) 机场参观

Setting: Hao Tao is a college student in NCIAE, who is going to fly to America for further education 1 month later. Right now he is talking with his friend Zang Tian, who works at Beijing Capital International Airport.

A: Hey, Zang Tian! I'm going to study in the United States in June. But I've no idea about civil aviation. Since you have been working there for several years, I hope you can do me a favor.

B: Sure, you've found the right person. We have arranged visitor tours at the airport, so it's very helpful for you to have a tour there.

A: Cool! But when is convenient for you?

B: What about next Thursday?

A: Fine, thank you.

Dialogue—Touring in the airport (2) Control Tower 机场参观

Look at these two pictures. What is that tower called and what is it used for? What are those people doing and where are they? Work with a partner to make at least two sentences for each picture.

B: Hao Tao, this is our terminal control tower, or tower for short.

A: Wow, it looks like a huge column from outside.

B: We control all the flights coming to and going out of the airport here.

A: Hey, I'm very proud of you. I guess you must be very busy.

B: Yeah, we are. It's our responsibility to control the aircraft movements safely.

A: I see, that's why people call you air police.

B: You are right.

Dialogue—Touring in the airport (3) Runway and Taxiway 机场参观

After listening to the dialogue please answer.

1. How many movements for an average day at this airport?
2. Does each scheduled flight have a time slot? What if they miss their time slot?

VOCABULARY ASSISTANT

time slot 时段

taxi (飞机起飞前或降落后的)滑行

fast-exit taxiway 快速出口滑行道

Dialogue—Touring in the airport (4) Apron 机场参观

While listening to this dialogue twice, please fill out the blanks below.

A: I've found there are several very big 1_____ connecting the taxiways.

B: Yes, they are aprons for 2_____ the aircraft.

A: I guess the biggest one is more than 3_____.

B: You're right. This is the main apron for 4_____. There are 5_____ on it, that is, it can hold 6_____ at the same time.

A: What about those smaller ones?

B: Some of them are for 7_____, and the others, for 8_____.

A: What are those vehicles busy doing on the passenger apron?

B: Some are 9_____, some are 10_____, some are 11_____, and some others are 12_____.

A: But I don't see many fueling trucks here.

B: Yes, since this is one of the most advanced airports in the world, we 13_____ with the fueling ports on the apron, which are linked to the fueling tubes underground.

A: Wow, I'm really proud of hearing that.

Unit 10 Touring, Shopping and Entertaining in Airport

✈ Dialogue—Touring in the Airport (5) Hangar 机场参观

Read the following dialogue with your partner and describe the hangar in your own words.

A: Hey, Zang, I've never seen such a huge building.

B: You're right. It's the biggest hangar in Asia. It's so big that it can hold 4 large-sized aircraft at the same time.

A: But I think you can repair your aircraft on the open apron.

B: Yes, we can do that way for lower level maintenance. But for overhauls and major repairs, we can't do outside. That's why we invested more than a billion RMB to build it in 1994.

A: Do you have so much work to do, I mean, can you recover your huge investment?

B: We can recover our investment within 10 years since we have so many aircraft to repair and we can do most of our maintenance at home.

A: So you have to send some of your aircraft abroad to repair them, right?

B: Not quite. We just send some parts and components abroad.

A: Can you tell me something about the operation of your company?

B: I'd like to. Our Aircraft Maintenance and Engineering Corporation, or AMECO for short, was set up in 1989 as a joint venture with Lufthansa Airline of Germany. We have introduced foreign capital, management and techniques from abroad in such a way that we have caught up with the advanced maintenance level of the world.

A: Congratulations on your success. I'm very happy to hear your introduction. Thank you.

VOCABULARY ASSISTANT

overhaul 彻底检修，大修　　　recover 重新获得
joint venture 合资
Lufthansa Airline of Germany 德国汉莎航空公司

✈ Dialogue—Touring in the Airport (6) Aircraft 机场参观

147

Listen to the dialogue and answer the following questions.

1. What are they talking about in this dialogue?
2. According to the dialogue, how many air routes and aircraft does our country have at present? Is it necessary to have more?

Shopping & Entertaining

Setting: Mr. Black is taking off in several hours to New York. Right now he is looking around in the airport with his wife.

Dialogue—Shopping & Entertaining at the Airport (1) At the Duty-free Store 机场购物及娱乐

Listen to the dialogues at the duty-free store and answer the following questions with your partner.

Questions

1. What type of perfume did Mr. Black buy for his wife? And how much is it?
2. What size shoes does Mr. Black's son wear?
3. What did Mr. Black buy and how much did he pay finally?
4. Besides ticket, what do you need to show to the seller when you want to buy something in a duty-free store at the airport?
5. What is the difference in shopping at a duty-free store comparing with an ordinary store?

VOCABULARY ASSISTANT		
perfume 香水	souvenir 纪念品	elegant 雅致的
price reduction 削价	discount 折扣	credit card 信用卡
drawback 退税	formality 手续	

Unit 10 Touring, Shopping and Entertaining in Airport

Dialogue—Shopping & Entertaining at the Airport (2) At the Restaurant
机场购物及娱乐

Listen to the dialogues twice and fill out the missing sentences below.

C: This is our menu. What can I do for you, sir?

P: I can't read the menu very well. 1_____?

C: Yes, our European food is very popular. We have all kinds of dishes and drinks.

P: 2_____.

C: No problem. We have all kinds of dishes and drinks.

P: Please tell me about some of your cuisines?

C: With pleasure. 3_____, and the typical ones are 4_____.

P: That sounds interesting. Tell me more about the two.

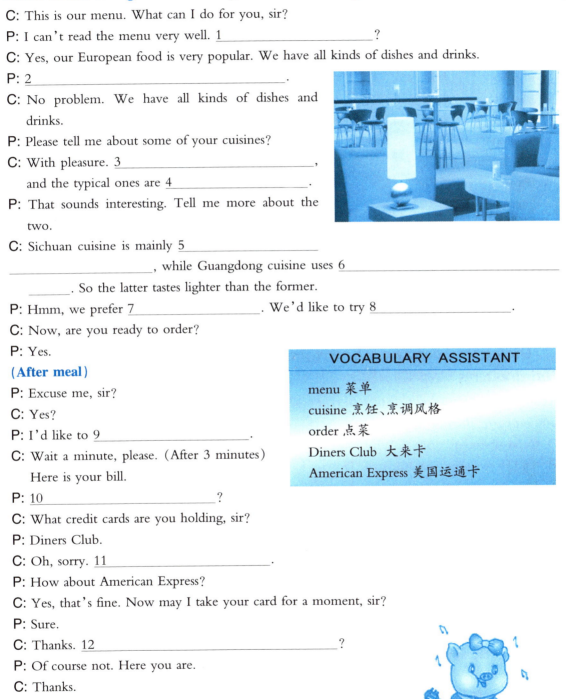

C: Sichuan cuisine is mainly 5_____ _____, while Guangdong cuisine uses 6_____ _____. So the latter tastes lighter than the former.

P: Hmm, we prefer 7_____. We'd like to try 8_____.

C: Now, are you ready to order?

P: Yes.

(After meal)

P: Excuse me, sir?

C: Yes?

P: I'd like to 9_____.

C: Wait a minute, please. (After 3 minutes) Here is your bill.

P: 10_____?

C: What credit cards are you holding, sir?

P: Diners Club.

C: Oh, sorry. 11_____.

P: How about American Express?

C: Yes, that's fine. Now may I take your card for a moment, sir?

P: Sure.

C: Thanks. 12_____?

P: Of course not. Here you are.

C: Thanks.

VOCABULARY ASSISTANT

menu 菜单
cuisine 烹饪、烹调风格
order 点菜
Diners Club 大来卡
American Express 美国运通卡

Information Bank

Expressions on Catering

Snack bar	快餐部	Black tea	红茶	Hot pepper	辣椒
Prawn	大虾	Cafeteria	自助餐厅	Green tea	绿茶
Beef Steak	牛排	Carp	鲤鱼	Bar	酒吧
Jam	果酱	Port chop	猪排	Fried rice	炒饭
Teahouse	茶馆	Butter	黄油	Ham	火腿
Steamed bread	馒头	Cafe	咖啡馆	Cheese	奶酪
Bacon	咸肉	Hamburger	汉堡包	Coffee	咖啡
Sugar	糖	Sausage	香肠	Spaghetti	意大利面条
Black coffee	不加奶咖啡	Salt	盐	Roast duck	烤鸭
Salad	沙拉	White coffee	加奶咖啡	Pepper	胡椒
Seafood	海鲜	Pudding	布丁		

Dialogue—Shopping & Entertaining at the airport（3）At the Barber's/Hairdresser's 机场购物及娱乐

Read this dialogue with your partner and then make another dialogue that takes place at the Barber's.

C: Good afternoon, madam. What can I do for you?

P: I'd like to change my hair style. Do you have any suggestions?

C: Sure. We do have some pattern books of hair styles, please have a look at them.

P: Oh, I like this one. I think it suits me.

C: That's pretty, indeed. But in my opinion, you would be more beautiful with short hair.

P: Really? But I'd like to have it sweptback.

C: Well, it's up to you. Anyway, I believe short hair is really suitable for you.

P: Hmm, I'm worried it will make me look strange.

C: Trust me. I'm sure you would look terrific if you had it done short.

P: Ok, let me have a try.

Unit 10 Touring, Shopping and Entertaining in Airport

Information Bank

hair style	发型	trim	整理,修剪	shampoo	洗发
sweptback	后掠式	crew cut	平头	bald head	秃头
pony-tail	马尾发型	cape	披肩发型	curly hair	卷发型
page boy style	娃娃头	straight hair	直发型	wave hair	大波浪型

center/central parting; part one's hair in the middle side parting; part one's hair on the left/right 中分头

Dialogue—Shopping & Entertaining at the Airport (4) At the Fitness Center 机场购物及娱乐

Listen to the dialogue and answer the questions below.

Answer the questions.

1. What do the Blacks do in the sports center?
2. What drink does Mr. Black order for himself?

Dialogue—Shopping & Entertaining at the Airport (5) At the Laundry 机场购物及娱乐

Read this dialogue with your partner and finish the exercise below.

C: Have you any laundry, sir?

P: Yes. I want to have my suit dry-cleaned.

C: Could you fill in the laundry list first, please?

(After 3 minutes)

P: Fine. Here is the list and my laundry bag.

C: Is there anything else that you want dry-cleaned?

P: No more. But I'd like my suit done before 4 p.m., I have to take off tonight.

C: No problem. We have an express laundry service. Leave it to me. I'll fix it.

P: Thanks. How much is the charge?

C: It's 50% extra for express service. That's RMB 80 in all.

P: All right.

151

Exercise—How to do laundry at home.

The following washing procedures are in disorder, please fill out the blanks with the words given below and put them into right order.

Words given:

sort	pour
pre-treat	choose
measure	start
according to	add

Step A: _____ your dirty clothes, making separate piles for whites, bright colors and darks. If you mix whites with colors in the wash, the colors may bleed onto and ruin your whites. Close zippers to prevent snagging, and empty pockets. _____ heavy stains with laundry detergent（清洁剂）or stain remover, heeding instructions on the product label.

Step B: _____ the soap into your washer or its detergent dispenser.

Step C: _____ your clothes, close the lid and let the machine do its work.

Step D: Close and turn on the dryer.

Step E: Use the measuring cap of the detergent bottle or the cup found in detergent boxes to _____ out the right amount of laundry soap _____ the manufacturer's instructions.

Step F: Once the clothes are completely dry, remove them from the dryer or drying rack and fold your clean laundry.

Step G: Put the clothes in the dryer after the wash is complete. Select the correct drying temperature for your laundry load: low for delicates, medium for most fabrics and high for cotton.

Unit 10 Touring, Shopping and Entertaining in Airport

Step H: _____ the water temperature for the wash cycle: hot, warm or cold. In general, use cold water to protect colors and darks from bleeding or fading, and to avoid shrinkage (缩水). Use warm or hot water for durable fabrics like cotton, and to ensure that your whites stay white.

Step I: _____ the washer before adding clothes, if you have time, to allow the detergent to dissolve in the water. The regular cycle suffices for most laundry, but use the gentle cycle for sheer or delicate fabrics. Adjust the water level to the size of your load.

The Right Order for washing at Home is: _____

Dialogue—Shopping & Entertaining at the airport (6) *At the bar* 机场购物及娱乐

Read the dialogue with your partner and make another dialogue that takes place in a bar by using the substitute words given below.

C: What can I offer you, sir?

P: A whisky, please.

C: OK, with or without ice?

P: With ice. And a non-alcoholic cocktail for my wife. By the way, could we have some nuts and snacks?

C: Certainly! I'll get a fresh supply for you. Wait a moment, please.

VOCABULARY ASSISTANT

whisky 威士忌   non-alcoholic 无酒精的
snack 快餐,小吃

Information Bank

Substitute words

white wine	白葡萄酒	red wine	红葡萄酒	mineral water	矿泉水
orange juice	桔子原汁	orangeade, orange squash	桔子水		
lemon juice	柠檬原汁	lemonade	柠檬水	beer	啤酒
cider	苹果酒	champagne	香槟酒	cocktail	鸡尾酒
liqueur	白酒, 烧酒	vodka	伏特加	brandy	白兰地

★ Further Reading 1

Airports

Airports provide air transportation for people, freight, mail, perishable foods, and other important items. To achieve this, an airport is used for the landing and takeoff of aircraft. An airport is composed of several areas and buildings that are designed to serve the needs of both passengers and aircraft.

Runways are the long, narrow concrete areas where airplanes take off and land. Taxiways are concrete roads that aircraft follow from the runways to the terminal building. The terminal building also contains ticket and baggage counters. The control tower is located near the terminal building. From this tower, air traffic control coordinates aircraft movements both in the air and on the ground. For security purposes, access to major airports is usually limited to special roads. Many airports have large car parking areas on the ground or in multistory car parks.

Airports are among the busiest transportation centers in a region. The business they created is vital to the world economy and individual national economies. Airports are so important to a city that many companies will not locate factories or offices in cities that do not have an adequate airport. There are three major types of airports: military, general aviation, and commercial airports. Airports differ in size and layout depending on their function and the types of aircraft and traffic that use them.

Military airports have one or two paved runways, generally 3,000 to 4,600 meters long, or

Unit 10 Touring, Shopping and Entertaining in Airport

10,000 to 15,000 feet long. These airports are used only by military aircraft. General aviation airports cater for small civil aircraft and are smaller than commercial airports. They are often located in rural areas or in small towns. General aviation airports have one or two runways from 900 to 1,500 meters long, or 3,000 to 5,000 feet long. Commercial airports are used by airlines. These airports may be small or large. Small commercial airports have one or two runways from 1,800 to 2,400 meters long. Large commercial airport usually have pairs of parallel runways from 3,000 to 3,700 meters in length.

VOCABULARY ASSISTANT

freight 货物　　　　　　　perishable food 易腐食品
military airport 军事机场　　commercial airport 商务机场
general aviation airport 专用航空机场

Over to you

1. What is an airport?
2. How many types of airports and what does each type cater for?

★ Further Reading 2

The Airport Terminal Buildings

The airport terminal building provides all major passenger services, such as ticket sales, passenger check-in, baggage handling, and security check.

A terminal can be organized in several different ways. The four different types of terminals are gate arrival, pier, satellite, and transporter. All major terminals provide the same sort of services. Each type connects passengers with aircraft in different ways.

Gate arrival terminals are rectangular buildings that have aircraft parking on one side and have car parking on the opposite side of the terminal. Simple gate arrival terminals are the most common type of terminal found at small airports.

Pier terminals have piers like arms that extend outward from a central building and provide boarding gates on both sides of each pier for its entire length of the terminal. The area around each pier is known as a concourse. Pier terminals provide efficient use of space, since common facilities can be located in the central building instead of at each gate. If a given airline has use of nearby gates, or an entire pier, then passengers transferring to other flights may not have far to walk.

Satellite terminals also provide common facilities at a centralized building. However, passengers need not walk the length of a pier. Instead, transportation to gate areas is provided by buses or by automated rail systems such as people movers. Satellite terminals are often circular in layout and provide aircraft parking around their entire perimeter. They have many of the same characteristics of pier terminals.

Transporter terminals use a common building for the processing of passengers, who then board specialized vehicles known as mobile lounges that ferry passengers directly from the gate to the aircraft and back. Transporter terminals work well for passengers on direct flights but are inconvenient for passengers who are transferring to other flights, since they can't simply walk to their connecting aircraft's gate. Nevertheless, the flexibility of transporter terminal system has made them popular at airports that have experienced rapid growth—the operators of such airports often find it easier to drive passengers to parked aircraft than to build an expensive new terminal.

Over to you

1. What is a terminal?
2. How many types of terminals?
3. What are they and what they are used for?

★ Further Reading 3

FITNESS! Why Do Yoga?

The short answer is that yoga makes you feel better. Practicing the postures, breathing exercises and meditation makes you healthier in body, mind and spirit. Yoga lets you tune in, chill out, shape up—all at the same time.

For many people, that's enough of an answer. But there's more if you're interested.

For starters, yoga is good for what ails you. Specifically, research shows that yoga helps manage or control anxiety, arthritis, asthma, back pain, blood pressure, carpal tunnel syndrome, chronic fatigue, depression, diabetes, epilepsy, headaches, heart disease, multiple sclerosis, stress and other conditions and diseases. What's more, yoga:

- Improves muscle tone, flexibility, strength and stamina
- Reduces stress and tension
- Boosts self esteem
- Improves concentration and creativity
- Lowers fat
- Improves circulation
- Stimulates the immune system
- Creates sense of well being and calm

Developed in India, yoga is a spiritual practice that has been evolving for the last 5,000 years or so. The original yogis were reacting, in part, to India's ancient Vedic religion, which emphasized rituals. The yogis wanted a direct spiritual experience—one on one—not symbolic ritual. So they developed yoga.

Yoga means "union" in Sanskrit, the classical language of India.

According to the yogis, true happiness, liberation and enlightenment comes from union with the divine consciousness known as Brahman, or with Atman, the transcendent Self. The various yoga practices are a methodology for reaching that goal.

Vocabulary

A

a shaving kit 一套剃须工具	Unit 4
academic conference 学术会议	Unit 3
accompanying adj. 偕行的	Unit 5
accuse v. 控告	Unit 4
affinity n. 类似；亲近性	Unit 9
aisle seat 靠过道的座位	Unit 2
alkali n. 碱金属	Unit 4
allowance n. 规定	Unit 3
American Express 美国运通卡	Unit 10
annoy v. 使烦恼、使生气	Unit 7
apprise v. 通知	Unit 9
apron n. 停机坪	Unit 10
assist v. 帮助	Unit 6

B

badge n. 标签	Unit 6
baggage check 行李牌	Unit 2
Bangkok International Airport 曼谷国际机场	Unit 9
Belgium 比利时	Unit 5
billiard adj. 台球的	Unit 4
book v. 预定	Unit 1
bother v. 打扰、麻烦	Unit 4
breakage n. 破损	Unit 3
briefcase n. 公文包	Unit 4
Brunei 文莱	Unit 5
buggy n. 婴儿车	Unit 6
buzz v. 嗡嗡作声	Unit 4

C

car battery 车用蓄电池	Unit 4
cardboard case 纸箱子	Unit 3
cargo compartment 货仓	Unit 2
catapults n. 弹弓	Unit 4
caustic soda 苛性钠	Unit 4
centimeter n. 厘米	Unit 3
certificate n. 证书	Unit 5
channel n. 通道	Unit 5
charge v. 收费	Unit 2
checked baggage 托运行李	Unit 3
check v. 托运	Unit 4
chess n. 象棋	Unit 7
cigarette n. 香烟	Unit 5
claim tag 认领牌	Unit 2
claim v. 申报	Unit 3
cloisonne n. 景泰蓝	Unit 3
coin n. 硬币	Unit 4
commercial airport 商务机场	Unit 10
concealed adj. 隐藏的，隐瞒的	Unit 4
confirmationed adj. 确定的	Unit 7
confiscate v. 没收，充公	Unit 5
connection n. 转机	Unit 3
container n. 箱、匣等容器	Unit 2
content n. 物品	Unit 2
control tower n. 机场指挥塔台	Unit 10
convenient adj. 方便的	Unit 3
conveyor belt 传送带	Unit 2
cooperation n. 合作	Unit 7
corkscrew n. 螺丝锥	Unit 4
corrosive n. 腐蚀剂	Unit 4

counselor *n.* 参赞	Unit 4
Courtesy Visa 礼遇签证	Unit 5
cover *n.* 封面	Unit 6
credit card 信用卡	Unit 10
creosote *n.* 碳酸	Unit 4
cue *n.* 球杆	Unit 4
cuisine *n.* 烹饪、烹调风格	Unit 10
customs clearance 结关,海关放行	Unit 9
Customs Declaration Form 通关申报表格	Unit 5
Customs *n.* 海关	Unit 5
cutlery *n.* 餐具	Unit 4
cyanide *n.* 氰化物	Unit 4

D

damage *n.* 损坏	Unit 3
dart *n.* 标枪,飞镖	Unit 4
declare *v.* 申报	Unit 5
definitely 确切地	Unit 8
delay *n.* 耽搁、迟滞	Unit 9
delicate *adj.* 易碎的	Unit 3
demented *adj.* 发狂的,精神错乱的	Unit 4
departure time 起飞时间	Unit 2
depart *v.* 启程,离开	Unit 1
deplane *v.* 下飞机	Unit 6
destination *n.* 目的地	Unit 2
deter *v.* 阻止	Unit 9
diarrhea *n.* 痢疾、腹泻	Unit 5
Diners Club 大来卡	Unit 10
Diplomatic immunity 外交赦免权	Unit 4
diplomatic Visa 外交签证	Unit 5
diplomat *n.* 外交人员	Unit 4
discount *n.* 折扣	Unit 10
dose *n.* 剂量	Unit 5
double-entry 二次入境	Unit 5
drawback *n.* 退税	Unit 10
duty *n.* 税	Unit 5

E

effective *adj.* 有效的,其作用的	Unit 5
efficient *adj.* 有效的	Unit 9
elegant *adj.* 雅致的	Unit 10
emergency exit 紧急出口	Unit 6
empty *v.* 清空,倒空	Unit 4

ensure *vt.* 确保	Unit 3
entry card *n.* 入境卡	Unit 5
entry *n.* 入境	Unit 5
escort *v.* 伴随	Unit 6
estimate *v.* 估计	Unit 7
exceed *v.* 超出	Unit 3
excess baggage 超重行李	Unit 2
exempt *adj.* 被免除的	Unit 4
exit *n.* 出境	Unit 5
expedite *v.* 加速	Unit 9
expire *v.* 期满	Unit 5
extent *n.* 限度、范围	Unit 7
eyebrow tweezers 眉毛夹	Unit 6

F

fare *n.* 费用	Unit 1
fast-exit taxiway 快速出口滑行道	Unit 10
fax *v./n.* 传真	Unit 9
finalize *v.* 定稿,定案	Unit 1
first class 头等舱	Unit 3
flammable *adj.* 易燃的	Unit 4
flight number 航班号	Unit 1
for the sake of 出于……的原因	Unit 3
formality *n.* 手续	Unit 10
formality *n.* 手续	Unit 5
freight *n.* 货物	Unit 10
frequency *n.* 频率	Unit 4
frustrating *v.* 令人沮丧的	Unit 7

G

gas cylinder 毒气筒	Unit 4
general aviation airport 专用航空机场	Unit 10
gilm *n.* 胶卷	Unit 4
ground staff 地勤人员	Unit 6
guardian *n.* 监护人	Unit 6

H

hand carry baggage 手提行李	Unit 3
handle *v.* 对待;处理	Unit 3
hangar *n.* 机库	Unit 10
hesitate *v.* 犹豫	Unit 6
hijacking *n.* 劫机	Unit 4

hike v. 远足		Unit 4
hypodermic needles n. 皮下注射器针头		Unit 4

I

identify v. 识别出	Unit 6
Immigration Hall 入境大厅	Unit 5
implement v. 贯彻,执行	Unit 4
improperly adv. 不适当地	Unit 3
individual adj. 单独的	Unit 6
inducement n. 引诱,动机	Unit 9
infant n. 婴儿	Unit 6
infectious adj. 有传染性的	Unit 4
infirmary n. 医务室	Unit 5
inform v. 通知、告知	Unit 3
injection n. 注射	Unit 5
inspect v. 检查	Unit 5
intern n. 实习	Unit 5
irregularity n. 不规则,无规律	Unit 9
issue n. 问题	Unit 6

J

jaundice n. 黄疸	Unit 5
joint venture 合资	Unit 10

K

keep my fingers crossed 祈祷能够成功	Unit 7
Kenya 肯尼亚	Unit 5

L

label n. 标签	Unit 2
laptop computer 手提电脑	Unit 8
lighter n. 打火机	Unit 4
Limited Release Tag 免除责任行李牌	Unit 3
limit n. 限制	Unit 3
loaded adj. 装好胶卷的	Unit 4
locate v. 查找……的地点,定位	Unit 9
long distance call 长途电话	Unit 7
lounge n. 配有沙发的休息厅	Unit 6
Lufthansa Airline of Germany 德国汉莎航空公司	Unit 10
Luxemburg 卢森堡	Unit 5

M

magnet n. 磁铁	Unit 4
magnetron n. 磁电管	Unit 4
maintenance mechanic 机械师	Unit 4
mark v. 做标记	Unit 5
maximum n. 最大量	Unit 3
maximum adj. 最大限度的	Unit 3
maximum n. 最高	Unit 6
mechanical adj. 机械的	Unit 7
medication n. 药物治疗	Unit 5
menu n. 菜单	Unit 10
mercury n. 汞	Unit 4
military airport 军事机场	Unit 10
minimum n. 最低	Unit 6
miscarry v. 被误送	Unit 9
multiple-entry 多次入境	Unit 5

N

nationality n. 国籍	Unit 5
needle n. 针	Unit 6
Netherlands 荷兰	Unit 5
non-alcoholic adj. 无酒精的	Unit 10
normally adv. 通常地	Unit 2
not...any longer 不再	Unit 5

O

oiled paper 油纸	Unit 4
order v./n. 点菜	Unit 10
ordinary Visa 普通签证	Unit 5
overhaul n./v. 彻底检修,大修	Unit 10
overweight n. 超重	Unit 3
owing to 由于	Unit 7
oxidiser n. 氧化物	Unit 4

P

package n. 旅行社代办的旅游	Unit 9
pack n. 包装	Unit 3
passport n. 护照	Unit 5
perfume n. 香水	Unit 10
perishable food 易腐食品	Unit 10

permanently *adv.* 永久地	Unit 5	
peroxide *n.* 过氧化物	Unit 4	
pet *n.* 宠物	Unit 2	
phonetic letter 拼音字母	Unit 5	
pilot *n.* 飞行员	Unit 4	
pin *n.* 别针	Unit 6	
pistol *n.* 手枪	Unit 4	
platform *n.* 平台	Unit 4	
policy *n.* 政策	Unit 6	
pool *n.* 撞球	Unit 4	
pool *v.* 共有、共享、联营	Unit 3	
portable typewriter 便携式打印机	Unit 3	
Portugal 葡萄牙	Unit 5	
potter's knife 陶瓷刀	Unit 4	
price reduction 削价	Unit 10	
proof *n.* 证明	Unit 6	
provided *conj.* 假设、倘若	Unit 5	
purpose *n.* 目的	Unit 5	

Q

quarantine inspection 检疫检查	Unit 2
quarantine *n.* 检疫	Unit 5
quicklime *n.* 生石灰	Unit 4

R

radioactive *adj.* 放射性的	Unit 4
reasonable *adj.* 适当的	Unit 3
receipt *n.* 收据	Unit 5
recognition *n.* 承认	Unit 7
recover *v.* 重新获得	Unit 10
redo *v.* 重做	Unit 3
reduce *v.* 减少	Unit 3
refuse *v.* 拒绝	Unit 4
region *n.* 地区	Unit 5
regulation *n.* 规定	Unit 3
reimbursement *n.* 付还,退还	Unit 9
relax *v.* 放松	Unit 6
remind *v.* 提醒	Unit 3
renew *v.* 更新	Unit 5
rent *v.* 租用	Unit 9
replica *n.* 复制品	Unit 4
Republic of Korea 韩国	Unit 5
reservation *n.* 预订,预约	Unit 1

responsible *adj.* 负责任的	Unit 8
restriction *n.* 规定	Unit 6
retain *v.* 保存	Unit 5
roll up 卷起	Unit 5
runway *n.* 跑道	Unit 10

S

schedule *n.* 安排	Unit 8
scissor *n.* 剪刀	Unit 4
seal *v.* 密封	Unit 3
senior flight attendant 乘务长	Unit 6
service Visa 公务签证	Unit 5
sharp *adj.* 尖的	Unit 6
shelf *n.* 架子	Unit 8
shorten *v.* 缩短	Unit 9
single-entry 一次入境	Unit 5
sleeve *n.* 袖子	Unit 5
snack *n.* 快餐,小吃	Unit 10
snooker *n.* 桌球	Unit 4
sort *vt.* 整理	Unit 6
souvenir *n.* 纪念品	Unit 4
special local product 特产	Unit 5
spirits *n.* 烈酒	Unit 5
srsenic *n.* 砷	Unit 4
standard *n.* 标准	Unit 7
sticker *n.* 标签	Unit 3
strap *n.* 带子	Unit 3
strict *adj.* 严格的	Unit 3
strictly *adv.* 严格地	Unit 3
sub-categories 子种类	Unit 5
submit *v.* 服从	Unit 5
supervision *n.* 监督、管理	Unit 6
symptom *n.* 症状	Unit 5

T

tag *n.* 标签	Unit 3
taxi *v.* (飞机起飞或降落后的)滑行	Unit 10
taxiway *n.* 滑行道	Unit 10
temporarily *adv.* 暂时地	Unit 5
terminal *n.* 航班的	Unit 7
the airport terminal sterile area 机场候机隔离区	Unit 4
thinner *n.* 稀释剂	Unit 4

161

threshold *n.* 跑道入口	Unit 10	valid *adj.* 有效的	Unit 5
thunderstorm *n.* 雷暴	Unit 7	visa *n.* 签证	Unit 5
ticket jacket folder 机票夹	Unit 2	volume *n.* 体积、容积	Unit 3
time slot 时段	Unit 10	volunteer *v.* 自愿(做、提供)	Unit 7
tobacco *n.* 烟草制品	Unit 5	vomit *v.* 呕吐	Unit 5
tour *v.* 旅行	Unit 5	voucher *n.* 凭单	Unit 7
toy *n.* 玩具	Unit 4		
trace *v.* 追踪	Unit 9	**W**	
track *v.* 跟踪	Unit 9		
transit *n.* 过境	Unit 5	weedkiller *n.* 除草剂	Unit 4
treat *v.* 对待;处理	Unit 3	wet cell 湿电池	Unit 4
tuberculosis *n.* 肺结核	Unit 5	whisky *n.* 威士忌	Unit 10
turn around 转过身	Unit 4	window seat 靠窗口的座位	Unit 2
tweezer *n.* 镊子	Unit 4	within one month 在一个月之内	Unit 4
U		**X**	
uncompanied *adj.* 无人伴随的	Unit 6	X-ray *n.* X射线	Unit 4
unexposed *adj.* 未曝光的	Unit 4		
United Airlines 美联航	Unit 4	**Y**	
V		yellow fever 黄热病	Unit 5
vaccination *n.* 接种疫苗	Unit 5		

Keys and Transcripts

Unit 1 Ticket Service

Step 1   Telephone Inquiry 电话咨询

1. This is the Booking Office of Air China
2. there are 18 flights going to Dali every week
3. the flight number
4. that departs at 1:40
5. the fare
6. make a reservation
7. not finalized

Match words and translations in the two columns.
1. B 2. K 3. L 4. G 5. A 6. D 7. J 8. E 9. F 10. H 11. C 12. I

Complete the following dialogue and practice with your partner.

1. I've booked an air ticket from Beijing to New York next Monday
2. I have to cancel the reservation
3. Could you tell me the flight number
4. Your name
5. I got it
6. You've booked the CA421 first class on next Monday, Sep. 27th
7. Would you like to book another flight
8. Thanks for calling. Good-bye Mr. Brown

Complete the following dialogue and practice with your partner.

1. Hello, how may I help you
2. Sure, where would you go
3. CA1314 takes off at 12:40 the day after tomorrow
4. CA542 takes off at 15:20 tomorrow. There are seats available. Would you like to take this flight
5. Here you are. By the way, do I need to pay again
6. Thanks for taking China Airlines

Unit 2 Check-in Service

Complete the following dialogue and practice with your partner.

1. May I have your ticket and ID Card
2. Please put your baggage on the conveyor belt
3. What kind of seat do you prefer
4. No more window seats are avaiable
5. here are your boarding pass and baggage check

Fill in the blanks with the given words.

1. check in   2. late   3. tickets and passports   4. baggage
5. the conveyor belt   6. overweight   7. the limit

Discuss in a small group and say something about the official documents that a passenger needs during the trip.

1. Passport   2. Visa   3. Travel Health   4. Ticket

Complete the following dialogue and practice with your partner.

1. What can I do for you
2. Can I check in now
3. The flight will depart at 9:30
4. Show me your ticket and passport, please
5. Have you got any baggage to check
6. Here are your ticket, passport, boarding card and baggage check

Read the above information carefully and show your partner how to use the check-in machine.

1. Step 1: to insert a credit card to identify youselves or by entering a flight confirmation number.
2. Step 2: to select your seat.

3. Step 3: to print out a boarding pass.
4. Step 4: to deliver your luggage at the nearest baggage drop-off point and proceed to the gate.

Unit 3 Baggage Check-in Service

Do you know the following restrictive provisions for check-in baggage at Beijing International Airport?

1. 5 kg   2. 20×40×55 cm   3. 7 kg
4. 20×40×55 cm   5. 115 cm

Work in pairs and complete the dialogue with your partner.

1. Good afternoon. Your ticket and passport, please
2. Do you have any baggage to check in
3. Would you put it on the scales
4. For a first-class passenger, the free baggage allowance is forty kilos
5. If the checked baggage is over the allowance, we will charge you for the overweight
6. You're welcome. Your boarding pass and baggage check, please

Rearrange the dialogue in the correct order.
d j f e k b a i h l c g

The following sentences could go together to form a full dialogue, but they are in the wrong order. Put them right.
f c i r d l n h o a p j q e g m b k

Translate the following useful sentences into English.

1. Do you have any baggage to check in?
2. Please put your bag on the scale. I'll weigh it.
3. Your baggage is 20 kilos. Passengers holding economy class ticket may carry 2 pieces within the total weight of 10 kg onto the plane. Your baggage is 10 kilos overweight. I'm afraid you will have to pay a charge for it.
4. The baggage allowance is different according to the class of your ticket.
5. Here is your receipt, ticket, passport, boarding pass and baggage check.

Complete the following dialogue with proper sentences given below.
d b e a c

Listen to the dialogue and fill in the blanks with the missing information while listening.

1. overweight   2. too long   3. length limited   4. free baggage allowance
5. length, width and height   6. overweight baggage   7. receipt

Translate the following sentences into English.

1. It's not within the free baggage allowance.
2. The sum of length, width and height should be no more than 158 cm.
3. This one is over the length limit.
4. Would you like to send it as unaccompanied baggage?
5. You have to pay 200 yuan as excess charge.

Complete the following dialogue and practice with your partner.

1. Have you measured it
2. This box is 92 cm long, 65 cm wide and 44 cm high
3. the sum of the length, width and height of each must not exceed 158 cm
4. Would you like to send the big box as unaccompanied baggage
5. You have to pay 25 Yuan as the excess charge

Complete the dialogue with the proper given words and practice with your partner.

checked baggage   change   claim   transfer   ship   your destination   connecting flight
take   transit lounge   wait for   label   interlined baggage   take care of

Read the following useful expressions and translate them into Chinese.

1. 按本公司规定,手提行李的重量和尺寸均被限定在一定的范围内
2. 确保所有旅客的安全和舒适
3. 确信你的行李包扎得很安全,适宜托运
4. 把行李直接托运至目的地

Unit 4 Security Check

Translate the following sentences into Chinese.

(1) 北京首都机场安全检查站欢迎您对我们的服务提出各种评论和建议。
(2) 拒绝接受安全检查的乘客不允许登机或进入机场候机隔离区域,并要承担此举所带来的任何损失。
(3) 请向机场地面服务部门咨询乘客托运行李的相关信息。

Translate the following sentences into Chinese.

1. 请打开您的数码相机,谢谢。
2. 先生,请您打开这瓶矿泉水并且喝一口,可以吗?
3. 安检工作要严格遵守高效检查、文明操作及礼貌服务的原则。

Keys and Transcripts

Please translate the following items into Chinese.

1. 安检的目的就是确保飞机和所有乘客的安全。
2. 根据新规定,这种物品是不允许乘客携带的。

Dialogue—Patrolling in the Airport Terminal Sterile Area 在机场候机隔离区巡逻

1. What about this one
2. Have you been checked, madam
3. She is going through the gate
4. Would you mind waiting inside the Departure Hall

Unit 5 Associated Examinations in Airport

The Customs at the Airport (1)

1. Have you anything to declare
2. What's the purpose of your visit
3. Would you mind opening this bag, please
4. What's inside the package
5. Got any tobacco? Spirits
6. Would you mind showing me your camera, please
7. May I see your customs declaration
8. Shall I have to pay duty on them
9. we'll just have to confiscate it

Match the two columns sentences and put them into right order to form a dialogue.

C. b. A. a. D. e. B. c. F. f. G. d. E

Translate the following sentences into Chinese.

1. 如果您持有如下物品,比如水果,辣椒,茄子,西红柿;动物尸体或样本;土壤;废弃的衣物,请您将这些物品交至检疫人员手中或丢入检疫箱中。
2. 根据我们的规定,人的血液制品及其相关产品是禁止带入中国境内的。

Dialogue—at the Frontier Inspection 边防检查

1. passport and entry card
2. not clearly noted on the visa
3. applied for
4. When my passport was returned
5. tour in Beijing
6. filled out

7. your passport will expire in 15 days

8. I need to renew my passport here in China

9. Have a pleasant stay in China and do remember to renew your passport

Unit 6 Service for Special Passengers

Listen to the following passage and try to get the answer to these two questions.

1. unaccompanied children
2. typical restrictions
3. traveling alone
4. at least one adult
5. five
6. twelve
7. proof
8. nonstop flights
9. higher minimum age
10. the last flight
11. 60 to 90
12. fees or other costs

Complete the following dialogue and practice with your partner.

1. Who will come to meet him at the airport
2. Now I'll seat him in a forward row so that our flight attendants find it easy to keep an eye on him
3. As his guardian, could you please read carefully and complete this Unaccompanied Minor form on the cover of the envelope
4. I'll put his passport, ticket and other travel documents in the envelope and pass it to our senior flight attendant on his flight
5. our ground staff at the airport will be informed of his arrival beforehand

Listen to the dialogue and complete the blanks.

1. would you like any assistance
2. he is not a passenger
3. We can arrange a wheelchair
4. our information counter
5. take you right on to your flight

Unit 7 Flight Irregularity

Complete the following dialogue.

1. What can I do for you
2. The flight is delayed
3. Because of poor visibility for today's morning
4. About two hours later
5. It's on the ground foor

Keys and Transcripts

Fill in the blanks with words given below. Change the form when necessary.

1. regret   2. delayed   3. inform   4. supplying   5. apologize   6. responsible
7. put   8. endorse, change

Rearrange the dialogue in the right order and practice with your partner.

b. g. l. q. o. j. m. a. d. r. i. h. e. p. c. n. k. f.

Complete the following dialogue with the given words and practice with your partner.

connect   maintenance   reservation   prefer   urgent   endorse   change   send   schedule   arrangements

Listen to the passage and fill in the blanks—Overbooking.

1. An airline, rail, or shipping company

2. miss the trip or don't show up

3. Business travellers

4. an oversale

5. give away their seats

6. free ticket or an upgrading

7. not refundable afterwards

8. Economy class

Unit 8 Other Services

Complete the following dialogue.

1. Yes. What's the problem?

2. I'm afraid not. Have you lost your passport?

3. Where exactly did you use your passport in the shop?

4. Well, let me call the suit-dress department to see if they've found a passport.

5. Sorry, your passport has not been found there, either.

6. You can fill in this lost property report, and I'll keep my eyes on it.

Listen and practice—Inquring about Flights 询问航班情况

1. Air China flight CA983

2. on Wednesday at 12:30 and Saturday at 15:15

3. 8:15 on Friday

4. About 18 hours

5. 2600 yuan

6. No, single

7. I'm happy to serve you

Listen and Practice—Inquiring about Traveler's Files 询问乘机所带证件

1. a domestic or an international
2. all your travel documents
3. reservation status
4. get your seat
5. connection
6. your health card
7. airport fee
8. All the international passengers
9. RMB 90
10. other procedures

Listen and practice—Inquiring about Boarding Formalities 询问乘机手续

1. Have you got your ticket
2. take a domestic flight or international one
3. Where are you going
4. a visa and your health card
5. go through all the formalities by yourself
6. pay your airport fee
7. the departure counter
8. check your baggage
9. a boarding pass
10. the passport control and the security check

Listen and practice—Inquiring about Flight Connection 询问转机

1. What can I do for you, sir
2. get your baggage
3. go through immigration
4. the airline desk to check in
5. security again

Listen and practice—Inquiring about Arrival Time 询问航班到港时间

1. The estimated time of arrival
2. 18:50
3. It has been delayed
4. 17:40
5. the Dispatching Office
6. 17:49

Listen and practice—Inquring about Flight Delay 询问晚点飞机情况

1. What's your flight number
2. due to heavy rain
3. the extent of the delay

4. the latest weather forecast

5. listen to the latest announcement about your flight

Listen and practice—Inquring about Charter Flight 询问包机

1. How many people are there in your team

2. When do you plan to go

3. it's hard for you to charter a flight

4. make your reservation two or three weeks earlier

5. make the reservation

Listen and practice—Inquiring about the Arrival Flight 询问航班到港情况

1. about 30 minutes   2. arrival gate   3. cleared customs

4. International Arrival Gate   5. You are welcome

Listen and practice—Inquring about Flight Connection 询问转机

1. Have you made a reservation for the flight to Qingdao

2. Would you show me your ticket please

3. reconfirm your reservation

4. that is necessary

5. Don't mention it

Listen and complete the dialogue.

1. Could you please spell passenger's full name for me

2. Just a moment   3. passenger namelist

4. 4:35   5. You are welcome

Unit 9 Arrival Passengers' Formalities

Match the explanations with the words below.

1. e   2. f   3. b   4. I   5. d   6. c   7. a   8. g   9. h

Domestic Passengers(3)国内旅客

1. go to the Jianguomen Hotel in the City

2. It does a circuit of the city hotels

3. large trunk which can carry all the baggage you can imagine

4. I need to mention that we don't take credit cards

5. the bus lounge

6. you have a pleasant stay in Beijing

International Arrival Baggage Claim (5) Baggage Damaged 国际旅客提取行李

1. it is scratched
2. this happened to your bag on Air China flight
3. have it repaired
4. your bag is irreparable
5. notify you immediately and offer you a new bag
6. the Irregularity Report
7. When the bag is repaired we'll deliver it to your hotel
8. apologize for any inconvenience this has caused you and look forward to having you fly with us again

International Arrival Baggage Claim (6) Compensating for Lost Baggage 国际旅客提取行李

Put the dialogue into right order and read it with your partner to know as a clerk how to deal with a passenger who has lost his baggage.

A 3 2 D 4 B 5 C 1

Unit 10 Touring, Shopping and Entertaining in Airport

Touring in the airport (4) Apron 机场参观

1. cement pavements
2. parking
3. 10 hectares
4. passenger aircraft
5. 80 stands
6. 80 large-sized aircraft
7. cargo handling
8. maintenance
9. loading or unloading baggage
10. cleaning the aircraft cabin
11. catering for the aircraft
12. filling fuel
13. refuel the aircraft

Shopping & Entertaining at the Airport (2) At the Restaurant 机场购物及娱乐

1. Can you give me some recommendations
2. But my wife wants to try some Chinese food
3. Chinese food is divided into eight most famous cuisines
4. Sichuan Cuisine and Guangdong Cuisine
5. made up of spicy and hot food
6. various kinds of seafood
7. seafood
8. Guangdong food
9. check my bill
10. Can I pay with a credit card
11. We don't accept it
12. Would you mind checking it and signing here

Exercise—How to do laundry at home

Step A: Sort, Pour;

Step B: Add;

Step C: Pre-treat;

Step E: measure, according to;

Step H: Choose;

Step I: Start.

Order: A E B I H C G D F

Transcripts

Unit 1 Ticket Service

Step 1 Telephone Inquiry 电话咨询

C: Hello. This is the Booking Office of Air China. Can I help you?

P: Yes, I need some information about flights to Dali.

C: Hold on for a second, please. Let me check. Hmm, there are 18 flights going to Dali every week. There are 4 flights on Monday and Tuesday, 2 on the other days. It's very convenient for you to fly there.

P: Yes, I think so. Could you tell me the flight number on Thursday afternoon?

C: The only flight is CA1849 that departs at 1:40 on Thursday.

P: By the way, how much is the fare to Dali?

C: RMB 1120. May I make a reservation for you?

P: Not now. My travel plans are not finalized. I'll make my reservation later. Thank you for the information.

C: When you are ready to book your flight, please remember Air China. We'll be happy to serve you. Good-bye.

Unit 2 Check-in Service

You may now check in for your flight from 48 hours to 2 hours before the scheduled departure time. We have numerous check-in options available to you, so whether you are at home, on your mobile, on the website, or even in downtown, you can check in when, where, and how it is convenient for you.

Online Check-in is a service that gives a possibility to check-in online to all passengers who have a ticketed reservation before arriving to the airport. Using the Web check-in is to avoid the queues at the airport. It is quite easy and convinient. In just two steps you are ready to go: select your seat using our seating plan and print your boarding pass before you leave for the airport. Passengers can enjoy check-in from 24 hours up to 90 minutes prior to the departure time.

Kiosk Check-in is an easy airport check-in for do-it-yourself type people. Passengers check themselves in using an automated machine (like an ATM machine). It offers passengers an elegant way to save time. It is operated by the passengers inserting a credit card to identify themselves or by entering a flight confirmation number. Then follow the instructions on the display, select seats—aisle or window and print out a boarding pass. A customer service phone is attached to the Kiosk if the passenger needs additional assistance from an airline attendant.

Keys and Transcripts

Unit 3 Baggage Check-in Service

Listen to the dialogue and fill in the blanks with the missing information while listening.

C: Hello, sir. Are you going to check in for flight XW105?

P: Yes. Here is my ticket.

C: Your ticket is OK. What baggage are you going to check?

P: I check these two cardboard boxes only.

C: Your small one is OK. But the other one is too big.

P: They only weigh 22 kg together, only 2 kg overweight.

C: I don't mean they are overweight too much. I mean that one is too long. Look, this is 120 cm long, 60 cm wide and 40 cm high. That one is 75 cm long, 40 cm wide and 30 cm high. The big one is over the length limited.

P: What's the limitation?

C: The free baggage allowance for each economy-class passenger is two pieces, and the sum of the length, width and height of each must not exceed 158 cm, but the sum of the length, width and height for the two pieces must not exceed 273 cm.

P: What should I do then?

C: The big box should be handled as overweight baggage. You should pay RMB 25.

P: OK, here is the money.

C: Here are your boarding pass, baggage checks and receipt for the overweight baggage.

P: Thank you very much.

Listen to the statement and complete the following information on baggage.

Baggage refers to personal property that passengers take on their travels. According to the transportation authorities, baggage carried by Air China can be classified as checked baggage and unchecked baggage.

Unchecked baggage should be suitable for placing into the closed overhead compartment or under the seat in front of passengers.

A. First and business class passengers are allowed two carry-on bags that cannot exceed 5 kg in weight.

B. Economy class passengers are allowed one carry-on bag that cannot exceed 5 kg (11 lbs) in weight and dimensions of 55 cm (21 inches) in length, 40 cm (15 inches) in width and 20 cm (7 inches) in height.

C. Baggage exceeding the above free baggage allowance should be checked.

—Maximum weight of each baggage should not exceed 45 kg, and the maximum dimension should not exceed $100 \times 60 \times 40$ cm^3. The baggage exceeding the above allowance should be transported as freight.

—Minimum weight of each baggage should not be less than 2 kg, and the minimum dimension should not be less than $30 \times 10 \times 20$ cm^3.

If the bags exceed the weight limit specified, the excess baggage charge per kilogram is 1.5% of the highest normal direct adult one way (Y class) fare.

Unit 4 Security Check

Checking with Hand Detector 用手提检测仪检查

One passenger is going through the gate of security check. As the bell buzzes, the agent has to stop him.

C: Excuse me, but do you still have any metal objects on you?

P: No. Nothing else.

C: Please stand here, on the platform...What's that?

P: Oh, I'm sorry. I just forgot this bunch of keys.

C: Please turn around...What's that in your hip pocket?

P: Oh, it's my lighter.

C: Could you take it out? That's all. You can leave now. Don't forget your luggage. Have a good journey.

Checking with Hand Detector用手提检测仪检查

C: Hello, sir. Please stand on the platform.

P: OK.

C: Oh, what's this?

P: A potter's knife.

C: Oh, let me see. What a sharp knife! According to the regulations in our country, this kind of knife is not permitted on the aircraft.

P: Really? I didn't know anything about it. But what can I do now?

C: You can leave it with us for safe keeping for no more than a month, or abandon it.

P: Then, please keep it for me till the next time I come here.

C: Well, I need your passport to write the receipt. Please sign your name here.

P: Thank you.

C: You're welcome. Just don't forget to come back within a month.

P: OK. Bye.

Checking Carry-on Luggage (1)

C: Good morning, sir. Do you have any unexposed film in this bag?

P: I don't think so.

C: Could you please put the bag on the conveyor belt, and your camera, too?

P: But my camera is loaded.

C: All right. We'll check it by hand. And could you please put your watch, keys and other metal articles in this tray? Now, walk through this gate and collect them at the other side over there.

P: All right.

C: Could you tell me what's in your bag, please?

P: Let me see. I've got some clothes, a shaving kit and some souvenirs.

C: Nothing else?

P: I don't think so.

C: Do you mind my opening it?

P: Not at all. Oh, there is an umbrella I forgot about.

C: That's what we saw on the scanning screen then. You know, we have to be careful. Sorry to have bothered you.

P: That's all right.

Checking Carry-on Luggage (2)

C: Excuse me, miss? Could you please empty your pockets of all the metal things and put them in this tray.

P: Including my keys and coins?

C: Yes, and please step over there.

P: All right. What shall I do now?

C: Please open your bags so we can check them. After that you can pick them up right behind that X-ray machine.

P: But I've got film in my bag.

C: That's all right. You can take it out if you wish, but this machine will not damage the film.

P: Fine. And this is my boarding pass.

C: Thank you for your cooperation, miss.

Checking Carry-on Luggage (3)

C: Is this your bag?

P: Yes.

C: Sorry, but we will have to open it for a further check.

P: OK.

C: Thank you. What's this?

P: Oh, these are my razor blades.

C: Sorry, it is not permitted to be taken on board according to the new regulations.

P: Oh, sorry. I didn't know the regulations. What should I do with it?

C: You could leave it with us until you come back. But you must come back within 30 days. Or you can abandon it.

P: OK. I'll abandon it.

C: That's OK. You may take your bag. Hope you enjoy your flight.

P: Thanks.

Checking Carry-on Luggage (4)

C: Sir, would you please put your handbag on this belt?

P: Yes, sir.

C: Have you got any lighter or keys with you?

P: Yes, I have.

C: Would you please put them in this tray and go through this gate?

P: Yes, sir.

C: What's in your bag? Would you mind my opening it?

P: No, sir. It's a toy pistol for my son.

C: Sorry, sir. According to the regulations, mimic weapons are not allowed to be taken into the passenger cabin.

P: Sorry, I didn't know that before. What shall I do with it now?

C: May I suggest that you check your handbag?

P: That's a good idea. Thank you.

C: You're welcome. Have a good trip!

Patrolling in the Airport Terminal Sterile Area

C: Whose briefcase is this?

P: It's mine.

C: What about this one?

P: Oh, it's also mine.

C: OK. Have you been checked, madam?

P: Yes. I'm waiting for my daughter. She is going through the gate.

C: I see. Would you mind waiting inside the Departure Hall? It's very crowded here.

P: Sorry, I'll go there.

Unit 5 Associated Examinations in Airport

The Customs at the Airport (1)

(As Mr. Wright has nothing to declare, he goes through the green channel. The customs agent is inspecting him.)

C: Good morning, sir. Are these your bags?

P: Yes, that's right.

C: Have you anything to declare?

P: No. I've only got clothes and things like that.

C: What's the purpose of your visit?

P: I'm here on business.

C: I see. Would you mind opening this bag, please?

P: Not at all.

C: What's inside the package?

P: Presents for some of my friends. They're Chinese glass vases.

C: Got any tobacco? Spirits?

P: I've got 100 cigarettes, but I haven't got any spirits.

C: Would you mind showing me your camera, please?

P: Not at all. Here it is.

C: Right, that's all. Thank you.

(Mrs. Wright has two bottles of perfume and she is asked to pay duty on them.)

C: May I see your customs declaration?

P: Oh, yes. Here you are.

C: Well, this is quite a list, isn't it?

P: Yes. I put down everything. I wonder if you have noticed that I have two bottles of perfume listed in the declaration. Shall I have to pay duty on them?

C: Yes, I'm afraid so.

P: And what will the duty on the perfume be?

C: It will be 40 dollars.

P: Oh, goodness. That's almost as much as I paid for the perfume.

C: I'm sorry. But the duty on perfume is very high.

P: Supposing I don't pay that much duty.

C: Well, we'll just have to confiscate it.

P: Oh, no. I think I'd better pay the duty. You see, it's my favorite perfume.

C: Even after you've paid the duty, I guess it's still cheaper than buying it locally.

P: Yes, I suppose so.

At the Frontier Inspection

C: Morning, madam. Please show me your passport and entry card.

P1: Here you are.

C: How many kids do you have with you?

P1: Only one. His name is on my passport.

C: But his name is not clearly noted on the visa, why?

P1: Really? Sorry, I have no idea about the reason. I had applied for both of us. When my passport was returned, I thought everything was OK.

C: Please wait for a moment. We'll investigate it, and be back at once.

C: Hello, sir. May I see your passport, please?

P2: Here you are.

C: Do you come to China alone?

P2: No, my wife and my son are with me to tour in Beijing.

C: You come here just to tour in Beijing only?

P2: Not exactly. We come to Beijing but we'd like to visit Shanghai as well.

C: I see. Have you filled out the entry cards?

P2: Yes, I have. Have you looked at them?

C: Yes, but I should mention one thing; your passport will expire in 15 days.

P2: Yes, I know. But I didn't think of it until we left New York.

C: Then, you are going back to New York, aren't you?

P2: Yes, that's true. I need to renew my passport here in China. Thank you.

C: You are welcome. Have a pleasant stay in China and do remember to renew your passport.

P2: Thank you. Bye.

Unit 6 Service for Special Passengers

Listen to the following passage and try to get the answer to these two questions.

Most airlines allow unaccompanied children to fly, though usually with several restrictions. Programs vary widely from airline to airline, and no two airlines will have the same polices. This brief overview will discuss the typical restrictions of these programs as well as a number of issues that you may want to address before allowing a child to travel unaccompanied.

While a child traveling alone is considered an unaccompanied child by the airlines, a group of children would be considered unaccompanied if there is not at least one adult traveling with them.

Most airlines have a minimum age for unaccompanied children, typically five, and a maximum age, typically 12. You or your child may be asked to provide some kind of proof of the child's age, so be prepared to bring appropriate documentation to the airport.

For unaccompanied children traveling under the airline's supervision, there may be additional restrictions and requirements. Typical requirements and restrictions may include the following:

- Allowing unaccompanied children only on nonstop flights
- Having a higher minimum age if the child is on a flight requiring a change of aircraft or a change of flight number
- Not allowing unaccompanied children on the last flight of the day for that destination
- Not allowing unaccompanied children on flights that involve a second carrier
- Requiring earlier check in, typically 60 to 90 minutes before departure
- Charging adult fees or other costs associated with the service for unaccompanied children

Listen to the dialogue and complete the blanks.

C: Miss, would you like any assistance?

P: No, thank you just the same. My son has come to see me off and he will assist me.

C: I'm afraid he is not allowed to enter Immigration and Customs areas because he is not a passenger.
P: Oh, I didn't think of that. Then, I will need your special assistance.
C: We can arrange a wheelchair if you would like one.
P: Yes, I would.
C: Miss, our agent will meet you at our information counter just over there at 11:00 a.m., one hour before flight departure. The agent will be wearing a uniform like mine. He will take you right on to your flight.
P: Thank you.

Unit 7 Flight Irregularity

Overbooking is a term used to describe the sale of access to a service which exceeds the capacity of the service. An airline, rail, or shipping company can book more customers onto a vehicle than can actually be accommodated by an aircraft, train, or cruise ship. This allows them to have a (nearly) full vehicle on most runs, even if some customers miss the trip or don't show up (tickets are often rebookable afterwards). Business travellers often cancel at the last minute, when their meetings take more time than planned. If everyone shows up, at least in the case of airlines, the overbooking will cause an oversale. Airlines may ask for volunteers to give away their seats, and/or refuse boarding to certain passengers, in exchange for a compensation that may include an additional free ticket or an upgrading in a later flight. They can do this and still make more money than if they booked only to the plane's capacity and had it take off with empty seats. Some airlines do not overbook as a policy that provides incentive and avoids customer disappointment. They have mostly tourists and their tickets are not refundable afterwards, so their passengers show up. A few airline frequent flyer programs actually allow a customer the privilege of flying an already overbooked flight; another customer will be asked to leave. Often only Economy class is overbooked while higher classes are not, allowing the airline to upgrade some passengers to otherwise unused seats.

Unit 8 Other Services

Listen and Practice—Inquring about Flights 询问航班情况
C: Hello. Can I help you?
P: Yes, I plan a trip to New York next week. Are there any direct flights from Beijing to New York?
C: Wait a moment please. I will check the exact schedule for you. (a moment later) Air China flight CA983 is scheduled on Wednesday at 12:30 and Saturday at 15:15.
P: Are there any extra flights during the Olympic games?
C: Yes. Flight CA531 departs at 8:15 on Friday.

P: What's the flying time between Beijing and New York?

C: About 18 hours.

P: How much is the ticket?

C: 2600 yuan.

P: Return?

C: No, single?

P: By the way, is that a Boeing 747 flight?

C: Yes. It's a Boeing 747~400.

P: That's all I want to know. Thank you!

C: You're welcome. I'm happy to serve you.

Listen and Practice—Inquiring about Traveler's Files 询问乘机所带证件

P: Good morning, Miss. This is my first time to travel by air. I don't know the procedures I have to go through before boardng.

C: The procedures you have to go through depend on whether you are a domestic or an international passenger.

P: Oh, I think I am an international passenger. I'll take flight MU559 to Madrid this evening.

C: Have you got all your travel documents with you?

P: I think so. I have got my passport, and the ticket.

C: What about the reservation status on your ticket? Would you please show me your ticket?

P: Yes, here you are.

C: Good, your reservation status is OK.

P: What does that mean?

C: That means you can get your seat on that flight. If your reservation status is RQ, especially when you make a connection you cannot get your seat on the flight. RQ means your reservation is only requested but not confirmed.

P: Oh, I see. Anything else?

C: Have you got your health card?

P: Oh, yes. Here it is.

C: OK! Have you paid your airport fee?

P: What, airport fee?

C: Yes. All the international passengers leaving from any airport within China should pay RMB 90 for airport fee. You should pay it first. And then you can go through other procedures.

P: OK, I'll pay it first. Thanks a lot.

Listen and Practice—Inquiring about Boarding Formalities 询问乘机手续

P: Excuse me. This is my first time to travel by air. There are so many people standing in lines. I feel very confused. I don't know which line I should stand in.

C: Have you got your ticket?

P: Yes. Here you are.

C: Are you going to take a domestic flight or international one?

P: International flight.

C: Where are you going?

P: I'm going to New York.

C: Have you got your passport with a visa and your health card?

P: Yes, here they are. Can you deal with all the formalities for me?

C: No, I can't. I just want to know whether they are by ready. You have to go through all the formalities by yourself.

P: I see.

C: OK! All your travel documents are ready. Now, please go there and pay your airport fee first, and then go into the departure counter to check in for your flight, and check your baggage. After this, you'll get a boarding pass. Then you should follow other passengers to go through the passport control and the security check. When it's time to board the plane, you may board your flight.

P: Thank you for your help.

Listen and Practice—Inquiring about Flight Connection 询问转机

C: What can I do for you, sir?

P: Oh, yes. My flight just landed at 6:50 a.m. and my KLM flight leaves at 8:40 am. I was wondering if this is enough time to get my bags from my flight to Boston and to hop on the flight to AMS? If there isn't enough time, I'll have to cancel my next flight.

C: You have nearly 2 hours, and you may need it. It's a hig airport for sure. Let me show you. If you are changing airlines you'll probably need to get your baggage, then go through immigration, then get to the airline desk to check in to the flight to AMS, then go through security again.

P: Oh, my God! I'm not sure whether I'll have to change airlines. Can you help me check?

C: Of course, sir. Yes, they are different airlines. But, let me see...Luckily, sir, you don't have to change airline because they are partner airlines.

P: You mean...?

C: Things are getting easier now. Your bags should go straight through and you should not have to clear customs.

P: Take your time, sir, and enjoy your stay at the airport.

Listen and Practice—Inquiring about Arrival Time 询问航班到港时间

P: Good moring, miss. Can you tell me the arrival time of flight XW102 from Kunming, please? The scheduled time of arrival of XW102 is 17:20, but it's already 18:00.

C: Yes. The estimated time of arrival will be 18:50. The weather in Changsha is not good. It has been delayed.

P: That's too bad. We have a delegation on that flight. And our cars have been waiting outside the termial building for half an hour.

C: I am sorry that your cars have to wait for about 1 more hour.

P: By the way, can you tell me the departure time of CA906 at Kunming? We have another delegation on that flight.

C: Well, its estimated time of departure is 17:40, but I don't know its actual time of departure. I have to ask the Dispatching Office. Would you please wait a moment?

...

OK! Its actual time of departure is 17:49.

P: Many thanks for your help.

Listen and Practice—Inquring about Flight Delay 询问晚点飞机情况

P: Excuse me, miss.

C: What can I do for you?

P: I've just heard an announcement that my flight has been delayed.

C: What's your flight number?

P: Flight MU530 to Seattle.

C: Yes, it's true. It has been delayed.

P: Could you please tell me why?

C: Yes, of course. The delay is due to heavy rain.

P: How long will the delay be? Do you have any further information about it?

C: I am sorry, we don't know the extent of the delay at present. But according to the latest weather forecast, there will be a change in the weather soon.

P: We have to wait. Well, is it possible for the rain to stop before noon?

C: It's hard to say. Weather is so changeable in the summer. Please listen to the latest announcement about your flight.

P: Yes, I will. Thanks a lot. Bye!

C: Bye!

Listen and Practice—Inquring about Charter Flight 询问包机

C: Hello. Can I help you?

P: Yes, I'm the leader of the French football team. We have already finished our match. We would like to charter a flight to go back to Paris.

C: How many people are there in your team?

P: We have 50 people, including the coaches and players together with some sportswear and sports equipment.

C: When do you plan to go?

P: Next Tuesday.

C: It's Friday today. There are only 3 days left. I think it's hard for you to charter a flight at such short notice. During the Olympic Games, there are many charter flights. You had better make your reservation two or three weeks earlier. But you can have a try.

P: I think so. Where can I charter a flight?

C: You should go to Air China Booking Office to make the reservation.

P: Where is the Air China Booking Office?

C: On the second floor of the terminal building, east side.

P: Thank you for your help.

C: You're welcome.

Listen and Practice—Inquiring about the Arrival Flight 询问航班到港情况

P: Will you please tell me where to go to meet flight MU548 from Bangkok arriving at 7:50 p.m.?

C: Well, about 30 minutes after the flight has landed the passengers will be coming through the arrival gate having cleared customs.

P: About 30 minutes?

C: Yes. International Arrival Gate on the first floor.

P: Thank you very much.

C: You are welcome.

Listen and Practice—Inquring about Flight Connection 询问转机

P: Excuse me.

C: Yes, sir. Can I help you?

P: I've just arrived from San Francisco and I'm going to fly to Qingdao to watch the Olympic canoeing contest. How can I make my connection?

C: Have you made a reservation for the flight to Qingdao?

P: Yes, I have. MU433.

C: Would you show me your ticket please?

P: Here is my ticket.

C: You should reconfirm your reservation at the Domestic Transfer Booking Office.

P: Where is the Domestic Transfer Booking Office?

C: On the second floor, east side.

P: By the way, so I have to claim and transfer my baggage?

C: Yes, that is necessary.

P: I see. Sorry to have given you so much trouble.

C: Don't mention it.

Listen and Practice—Passenger Enquiries 乘机旅客查询

Setting: At China Eastern Airline Information Desk Shanghai Hongqiao Airport

P: Would you please tell me if Mr. Wang Qiang is arriving on your flight from Madried today?

C: I'll be glad to check that for you. Could you please spell passenger's full name for me?

P: W-A-N-G Q-I-A-N-G.

C: Just a moment.

...

C: I show a Wang Qiang on the passenger namelist for MU552, which will arrive in Shanghai at 4:35 this afternoon.

P: Flight MU552 and it gets in at 4:35 p.m. Thank you.

C: You are welcome.

Unit 9 Arrival Passengers' Formalities

Domestic Passengers(3)国内旅客

Mr. Wang and his team are going to the shuttle bus counter at the airport.

C: What can I do for you, sir?

P: I want to go to the Jianguomen Hotel in the City. Do you go there?

C: Yes, we have a bus leaving in 10 minutes. It does a circuit of the city hotels. The Jianguomen Hotel is the 4th stop. It takes about an hour.

P: That sounds good. We have a lot of baggage. Could you manage that?

C: Sure. The bus has a large trunk which can carry all the baggage you can imagine.

P: How much does it cost?

C: It's RMB 30. That's much cheaper than a taxi. But I need to mention that we don't take credit cards.

P: I'm happy with that. Thanks.

C: OK, please wait in the bus lounge and the driver will call you when the bus is ready to leave. I hope you have a pleasant stay in Beijing.

International Arrival Baggage Claim (5) Baggage Damaged

P: Sir, my bag has just come out of the conveyor belt and I find it is scratched.

C: I'm terribly sorry this happened to your bag on Air China flight.

P: It was a new bag. I bought it not long before my departure.

C: Air China will have it repaired and return it to you within 3 days. In the unlikely event that your bag is irreparable, we will notify you immediately and offer you a new bag. Is that acceptable to you?

P: OK.

C: Would you please fill out the Irregularity Report?

P: OK ... Here you are.

C: Thank you. When the bag is repaired we'll deliver it to your hotel. Once again, I would like to apologize for any inconvenience this has caused you and look forward to having you fly with us again.

Keys and Transcripts

Unit 10 Touring, Shopping and Entertaining in Airport

Touring in the Airport (3) Runway and Taxiway 机场参观

B: Look there! An aircraft of Air China is landing on the east runway.

A: How many aircraft land at the airport everyday?

B: Generally speaking, there are about 1500 movements for an average day.

A: Incredible. So many landings here per day?

B: Not quite, I'm afraid. A movement means either a take off or a landing.

A: Oh, got it. But how can you control them to take off and land in a good order?

B: For the scheduled flights, we have assigned a time slot for each of them to take off and land.

A: What if they miss their time slot?

B: Then they have to hold and wait until they are permitted to take off or land.

A: I'm fascinated. It seems to me that there must be a lot of runways here since you have so many aircraft moving on them.

B: No, by no means. Actually, we have only 2 runways here. The 2 that parallel to the runways are taxiways for aircraft taxiing on the ground. And the slanting ones between them are fast-exit taxiways.

A: But what do you mean by fast-exit?

B: Since there are so any movements at the airport, we can't let the aircraft stay on the runway for too long. The landing aircraft must leave the runway as fast as possible. Fast-exit taxiways are very useful for a busy modern airport like ours.

A: How interesting it is. I'd appreciate your introduction very much.

B: My pleasure.

Touring in the Airport (4) Apron 机场参观

A: I've found there are several very big cement pavements connecting the taxiways.

B: Yes, they are aprons for parking the aircraft.

A: I guess the biggest one is more than 10 hectares.

B: You're right. This is the main apron for passenger aircraft. There are 80 stands on it, that is, it can hold 80 large-sized aircraft at the same time.

A: What about those smaller ones?

B: Some of them are for cargo handling, and the others, for maintenance.

A: What are those vehicles busy doing on the passenger apron?

B: Some are loading or unloading baggage, some are cleaning the aircraft cabin, some are catering for the aircraft, and some others are filling fuel.

A: But I don't see many fueling trucks here.

B: Yes, since this is one of the most advanced airports in the world, we refuel the aircraft with the fueling ports on the apron, which are linked to the fueling tubes underground.

A: Wow, I'm really proud of hearing that.

Touring in the Airport (6) Aircraft 机场参观

A: Hey, Zang. I guess there are about 100 aircraft parking on the ground, right?

B: Yes and much more aircraft are flying in the sky.

A: All the aircraft are not the same. They are in various sizes, various colors and even various shapes.

B: Exactly. They are different types made by different manufactures.

A: How many types of aircraft are there in our country?

B: About 50 all together.

A: Do you think it's necessary to have so any different types of aircraft?

B: Yes, I do. At present, we have more than 1000 air routes in our country with different distances and different markets. So we need different types of aircraft to accommodate different market demands. This is very natural for market economy.

A: And how many aircraft are there in our country?

B: More than 500, I think.

A: It doesn't sound exciting. Don't you think we should have more?

B: Yes, I do. I hope we'll have more and more aircraft along with the fast development of our country.

A: So do I.

Shopping & Entertaining at the Airport (1) At the Duty-free Store 机场购物及娱乐

(at the counter)

C: Hello, what can I do for you, sir?

P: I'd like to buy a Chinese perfume for my wife as a souvenir.

C: I suggest this type of perfume. It has won a national super-quality certificate. It smells very elegant, doesn't it?

P: Yes, it does. How much is it?

C: 560 Yuan.

P: It's too expensive. Is there any price reduction?

C: Actually they are on sale now. Sorry, but we can't give you more discount. It's really inexpensive for its quality.

P: Well, I'll take it.

(at the cashier)

P: Please check my bill.

C: May I have a look at your ticket and passport, please? Will you pay by cash or credit card?

P: Cash, please. Could I see the bill? Well, what is this charged for?

C: It's the tax, sir.

P: May I have a receipt?

C: Sure, just a moment.

(at the counter)

P: Excuse me. I bought a pair of sports shoes for my son here just now. But my wife doesn't think the size fits him very well.

C: Let me see. OK. Do you want to change them or get your money back?

P: I'd like a pair of size 27.

C: Here you are.

P: Thank you very much.

(At the Drawback Office)

P: Good morning, sir. Can I go through drawback formalities here?

C: Yes, glad to help you. May I have a look at your receipt?

P: I've got 2 receipts. Here they are.

C: And your passport and ticket, please.

P: Hold on a second, please. Here you are.

C: Let me check. Your receipts amount to RMB 850. The tax rate is 8%. So we should return you RMB 66. Here you are.

P: But I don't think you are right.

C: Yes, I am, sir. You have to pay RMB 2 of service charge.

P: I see. Thank you very much.

C: You're welcome. Have a good time.

Shopping & Entertaining at the Airport (2) At the Restaurant

C: This is our menu. What can I do for you, sir?

P: I can't read the menu very well. Can you give me some recommendations?

C: Yes, our European food is very popular. We have all kinds of dishes and drinks.

P: But my wife wants to try some Chinese food.

C: No problem. We have all kinds of dishes and drinks.

P: Please tell me about some of your cuisines?

C: With pleasure. Chinese food is divided into eight most famous cuisines, and the typical ones are Sichuan Cuisine and Guangdong Cuisine.

P: That sounds interesting. Tell me more about the two.

C: Sichuan cuisine is mainly made up of spicy and hot food, while Guangdong cuisine uses various kinds of seafood. So the latter tastes lighter than the former.

P: Hmm, we prefer seafood. We'd like to try Guangdong food.

C: Now, are you ready to order?

P: Yes.

(After meal)

P: Excuse me, sir?

C: Yes?

P: I'd like to check my bill.

C: Wait a minute, please. (After 3 minutes) Here is your bill.

P: Can I pay with a credit card?

C: What credit cards are you holding, sir?

P: Diners Club.

C: Oh, sorry. We don't accept it.

P: How about American Express?

C: Yes, that's fine. Now may I take your card for a moment, sir?

P: Sure.

C: Thanks. Would you mind checking it and signing here?

P: Of course not. Here you are.

C: Thanks.

Shopping & Entertaining at the Airport (4) At the Fitness Center 机场购物及娱乐

C: Welcome, sir. We have the best fitness center in the city.

P: Do you have a yoga studio?

C: Of course. Would you like to do yoga?

P: My wife would. And do you have a swimming pool?

C: Yes, we do. Ours is a heated swimming pool.

P: Great! My wife will do the yoga, while I'd like to swim. By the way, can you offer drinks there?

C: Certainly. We have a cocktail bar, Hennessey XO and Martell VSOP and others. What would you like, sir?

P: Beer, please.

C: OK. I'll prepare everything for you.

P: Thanks.

Appendix

世界各国或地区主要航空公司代码
Codes of Airlines

Airline Code 二字码	Airline Company 公司英文名称	中文名	国家或地区
A			
AA	American Airlines	美国航空公司	美 国
AC	Air Canada	加拿大航空公司	加拿大
AE	Air Europe	欧洲航空公司	英 国
AF	Air France	法国航空公司	法 国
AH	Air Algeria	阿尔及利亚航空公司	阿尔及利亚
AJ	Air Belgium	比利时航空公司	比利时
AL	Allegheny Airlines Inc.	阿勒格尼航空公司	美 国
AM	Aero Mexico	墨西哥航空公司	墨西哥
AN	Ansett Airlines of Australia	澳大利亚安捷航空公司	澳大利亚
AQ	Aloha Airlines	阿罗哈航空公司	美 国
AR	Aerolineas Argentinas	阿根廷航空公司	阿根廷
AS	Alaska Airlines Inc.	阿拉斯加航空公司	美 国
AV	Aerovias Nacionales de Colombia	哥伦比亚国家航空公司	哥伦比亚
AY	Finn Air	芬兰航空公司	芬 兰
AZ	Alitalia	意大利航空公司	意大利
B			
BA	British Airways	英国航空公司	英 国
BF	Alert Bay Air Service Ltd.	阿勒特湾航空公司	加拿大
BI	Royal Brunei Airlines	文莱皇家航空公司	文 莱
BK	Okay Airways	奥凯航空公司	中 国
BL	BelAir-Belarussian Airlines	白俄罗斯航空公司	白俄罗斯
BR	Eva Airways	长荣航空公司	中国台湾
BT	Air Baltic	波罗的海航空公司	拉脱维亚
BY	Britannia Airways	大不列颠航空公司	英 国
B7	UNI Air	立荣航空公司	中国台湾

续表

Airline Code 二字码	Airline Company 公司英文名称	中文名	国家或地区
C			
CA	Air China	中国国际航空公司	中　国
CO	Continental Airlines	大陆航空公司	美　国
CP	Canadian Airlines International	加拿大国际航空公司	加拿大
CX	Cathay Pacific Airways	国泰航空公司	中国香港
CZ	China Southern Airlines	中国南方航空公司	中　国
D			
DL	Delta Air Lines	达美航空公司	美　国
DT	TAAG-Angola Airlines	安哥拉航空公司	安哥拉
E			
EA	Eastern Airlines	东方航空公司	美　国
EG	Japan Asia Airways（JAA）	日本亚洲航空公司	日　本
EI	Aer Lingus	爱尔兰航空公司	爱尔兰
EK	Emirats Airlines	阿联酋航空公司	阿拉伯联合酋长国
ER	DHL Airways	敦豪航空公司	美　国
ET	Ethiopian Airlines	埃塞俄比亚航空公司	埃塞俄比亚
EU	United Eagle Airlines	中国鹰联航空公司	中　国
EY	Etihad Airways	阿联酋联合航空公司	阿拉伯联合酋长国
EZ	Evergreen International Airlines	常青国际航空公司	美　国
F			
FG	Arianna Afghan Airlines	阿丽亚娜阿富汗航空公司	阿富汗
FI	Iceland Air	冰岛航空公司	冰　岛
FJ	Air Pacific	太平洋航空公司	斐　济
FM	Shanghai Airlines	上海航空公司	中　国
FR	Ryan Air	瑞安航空公司	爱尔兰
FX	Federal Express(Fed EX)	联邦快运公司	美　国
G			
GA	Garuda Indonesia Airways	印度尼西亚航空公司	印度尼西亚
GF	Gulf Air	海湾航空公司	巴　林
GM	Air Slovakia	斯洛伐克航空公司	斯洛伐克
GX	Air Antario	安大略航空公司	加拿大
G5	China Express Air	华夏航空公司	中　国
H			
HJ	Air Haiti	海地航空公司	海　地
HO	June Yao Airlines	上海吉祥航空公司	中　国
HP	American West Airlines	美洲西部航空公司	美　国
HX	Hong Kong Airlines	香港航空有限公司	中国香港
I			
IA	Iraq Airways	伊拉克航空公司	伊拉克

续表

Airline Code 二字码	Airline Company 公司英文名称	中文名	国家或地区
IC	Indian Airlines	印第安航空公司	印 度
IO	Air Paris	巴黎航空	法 国
IR	Iran Air	伊朗航空公司	伊 朗
IT	Air France Europe	法国欧洲航空公司	法 国
IW	AOM French Airlines	乌特雷默法国航空公司	法 国
IZ	Arkia Israel Inland Airlines	阿基亚以色列航空公司	以色列
J			
JD	Deer Air	金鹿航空	中 国
JK	Span Air	西班牙航空	西班牙
JL	Japan Airlines	日本航空公司	日 本
JS	Air Koryo	朝鲜航空	朝 鲜
J2	Azerbaijan Airlines	阿塞拜疆航空公司	阿塞拜疆
K			
KA	Hong Kong Dragon Air	港龙航空公司	中国香港
KE	Korean Airlines	大韩航空	韩 国
KL	KLM Royal Dutch Airlines	荷兰皇家航空公司	荷 兰
KM	Air Malta	马耳他航空公司	马耳他
KN	China United Airlines	中国联合航空公司	中 国
KQ	Kenya Airways	肯尼亚航空	肯尼亚
KU	Kuwait Airways	科威特航空公司	科威特
L			
LF	Fly Nordic	瑞典航空公司	瑞 典
LH	Lufthansa German Airlines	德国汉莎航空公司	德 国
LO	LOT Polish Airlines	波兰航空	波 兰
LX	Swiss Air	瑞士航空	瑞 士
LY	Israel Airlines	以色列航空	以色列
M			
MF	Xiamen Airlines	厦门航空公司	中 国
MH	Malaysia Airlines	马来西亚航空公司	马来西亚
MI	Silk Air	胜安航空	新加坡
MM	SAM Colombia	哥伦比亚麦德林航空公司	哥伦比亚
MJ	LAPA	阿根廷航空运输公司	阿根廷
MS	Egypt Air	埃及航空	埃 及
MU	China Eastern Airlines	中国东方航空公司	中 国
MX	Mexicana De Aviacion	墨西哥国际航空公司	墨西哥
N			
NB	JAS	日本佳速航空货运	日 本
NH	ANA All Nippon Airways	全日空航空公司	日 本
NQ	Orbi Georian Airlines	奥比格鲁吉亚航空公司	格鲁吉亚
NW	Northwest Airlines	美国西北航空公司	美 国

续表

Airline Code 二字码	Airline Company 公司英文名称	中文名	国家或地区
NX	Air Macau	澳门航空公司	中国澳门
NZ	New Zealand Airways	新西兰航空公司	新西兰
O			
OA	Olympic Airways	奥林匹克航空	希腊
OK	Czech Airlines	捷克航空公司	捷克
OQ	Chong Qing Airlines	重庆航空有限责任公司	中国
OS	Austrian Airlines	奥地利航空公司	奥地利
OV	Estonian Air	爱沙尼亚航空	爱沙尼亚
OZ	Asiana Airlines	韩亚航空公司	韩国
P			
PC	Fiji Air	斐济航空公司	斐济
PG	Bangkok Airways	曼谷航空公司	泰国
PK	Pakistan International Airlines	巴基斯坦航空公司	巴基斯坦
PR	Philippine Airlines	菲律宾航空公司	菲律宾
PS	Ukraine International Airlines	乌克兰国际航空公司	乌克兰
PT	Air Sweden	瑞典航空公司	瑞典
PZ	LAPSA Air Paraguay	巴拉圭航空公司	巴拉圭
Q			
QC	Air Zaire	扎伊尔航空公司	扎伊尔
QF	Qantas Airways	澳洲航空公司（澳大利亚快达航空公司）	澳大利亚
QI	Cimber Air	辛博航空公司	丹麦
QN	Royal Airlines	皇家航空公司	加拿大
QR	Qatar Airways	卡塔尔航空公司	卡塔尔
QZ	Zambia Airways	赞比亚航空公司	赞比亚
R			
RA	Royal Nepal Airlines	尼泊尔皇家航空公司	尼泊尔
RG	Varig Brazil	巴西航空公司	巴西
RJ	Royal Jordanian	约旦皇家航空公司	约旦
S			
SA	South African Airways	南非航空公司	南非
SC	Shandong Airlines	山东航空公司	中国
SD	Sudan Airways	苏丹航空公司	苏丹
SK	Scandinavian Airlines	北欧航空公司	瑞典
SQ	Singapore Airlines	新加坡航空公司	新加坡
SN	SABENA	比利时世界航空公司	比利时
SR	Swissair	瑞士航空公司	瑞士
SU	Aeroflot Russian Airlines	俄罗斯国际航空公司	俄罗斯
SV	Saudi Arabian Airlines	沙特阿拉伯航空公司	沙特阿拉伯
S8	EIK Airways	爱沙尼亚航空有限公司	爱沙尼亚

续表

Airline Code 二字码	Airline Company 公司英文名称	中文名	国家或地区
T			
TC	Indian Airlines	印度国家航空公司	印度
TG	Thai Airways International	泰国国际航空公司	泰国
TN	Australian Airlines	澳大利亚航空公司	澳大利亚
TK	Turkish Airlines	土耳其航空公司	土耳其
TO	Orient Thai Airlines	泰国东方航空公司	泰国
TP	TAP Air Portugal	葡萄牙航空	葡萄牙
TS	Turkmenistan Airlines	土库曼斯坦航空公司	土库曼斯坦
TU	Tunis Air	突尼斯航空公司	突尼斯
TW	Trans World Airlines Inc.	环球航空公司	美国
U			
UA	United Airlines	联合航空公司	美国
UL	Air Lanka	斯里兰卡航空	斯里兰卡
US	U. S. AIR	美国航空公司	美国
UY	Cameroon Airlines	喀麦隆航空公司	喀麦隆
V			
VG	VLM Airlines	维尔姆航空公司	比利时
VJ	Royal Air Cambodge	柬埔寨皇家航空公司	柬埔寨
VN	Vietnam Airlines	越南航空公司	越南
VP	VASP	圣保罗航空公司	巴西
VS	Virgin Atlantic Airways	维珍航空	英国
W			
WN	Southwest Airlines	西南航空公司	美国
WT	Nigeria Airway	尼日利亚航空公司	尼日利亚
WV	Air South Airlines	南方航空公司	美国
WY	Oman Air	阿曼航空公司	阿曼
W5	Tajikistan Airlines	塔吉克斯坦航空公司	塔吉克斯坦
Z			
ZH	Shenzhen Airlines	深圳航空公司	中国
3			
3U	Sichuan Airlines	四川航空公司	中国
4			
4J	Air Arabia	半岛航空公司	阿联酋
5			
5X	United Parcels Service(UPS)	联合包裹服务公司	美国
8			
8C	Eaststar Air	东星航空	中国
8L	Lucky Air	祥鹏航空	中国
9			
9C	Spring Air	春秋航空	中国

世界主要国家或地区及货币
Main Countries and Currencies

亚洲				
国家或地区		货币单位		缩写或符号
Afghanistan	阿富汗	Afghani	阿富汗尼	AFA
Brunei	文莱	Brunei Dollar	文莱元	B$
Burma	缅甸	Burmese Kyat	缅元	BUK
Cambodia	柬埔寨	Cambodian Riel	瑞尔	KHR
Cyprus	塞浦路斯	Cyprus Pound	塞浦路斯镑	CYP
China	中国	Renminbi Yuan	人民币元	CNY(¥)
Hong Kong	中国香港	H. K. Dollar	港元	HKD
India	印度	Indian Rupee	印度卢比	INR
Indonesia	印度尼西亚	Indonesian Rupiah	印尼盾	IDR
Iran	伊朗	Iranian Rial	伊朗里亚尔	IRR
Iraq	伊拉克	Iraqi Dinar	伊拉克第纳尔	IQD
Israel	以色列	Schelch	新谢克尔	NIS
Japan	日本	Japanese Yen	日元	JPY(¥)
Jordan	约旦	Jordanian Dinar	约旦第纳尔	JOD
R. O. Korea	韩国	Won	韩元	KRW
D. P. R. Korea	朝鲜	Won	朝鲜元	KPW
Kuwait	科威特	Kuwaiti Dinar	科威特第纳尔	KWD
Laos	老挝	Laotian Kip	基普	LAK
Lebanon	黎巴嫩	Lebanon Pound	黎巴嫩镑	LBP
Macao	中国澳门	Macao Pataca	澳门元	MOP
Malaysia	马来西亚	Malaysian Dollar	马来西亚元	MYR
Maldives	马尔代夫	Rufiyaa	马尔代夫卢比	MVR
Mongolia	蒙古	Tugrik	图格里克	MNT
Nepal	尼泊尔	Nepalese Rupee	尼泊尔卢比	NPR
Pakistan	巴基斯坦	Pakistan Rupee	巴基斯坦卢比	PKR
Philippine	菲律宾	Philippine Peso	菲律宾比索	PHP
Saudi Arabia	沙特阿拉伯	Saudi Arabian Riyal	沙特里亚尔	SAR
Singapore	新加坡	Singapore Dollar	新加坡元	SGD
Sri Lanka	斯里兰卡	Sri Lanka Rupee	斯里兰卡卢比	LKR
Syria	叙利亚	Syrian Pound	叙利亚镑	SYP
Thailand	泰国	Thai Baht	泰铢	BHT(฿)
United Arab Emirates	阿拉伯联合酋长国（阿联酋）	Dirham	迪尔汗	AED
Vietnam	越南	Vietnamese Dong	越南盾	VND

续表

欧洲			
国家或地区		货币单位	缩写或符号
Albania	阿尔巴尼亚	Albanian Lek	列克	ALL
Austria	奥地利	Europe Dollar	欧元	EUR(€)
Belgium	比利时	Europe Dollar	欧元	EUR(€)
Bosnia and Herzegovina	波斯尼亚和黑塞哥维那（波黑）	konvertibilna marka	波黑马克	BAM
Bulgaria	保加利亚	Bulgarian Lev	保加利亚列弗	BGL
Byelorussia	白俄罗斯	Rouble	白俄罗斯卢布	RBs
Croatia	克罗地亚	Croatia Kuna	克罗地亚库纳	HRK
Czech	捷克	Czech Koruna	捷克克朗	CZK
Denmark	丹麦	Danish Krone	丹麦克朗	DKK
Finland	芬兰	Europe Dollar	欧元	EUR(€)
France	法国	Europe Dollar	欧元	EUR(€)
Germany	德国	Europe Dollar	欧元	EUR(€)
Great Britain	英国	Pound	英镑	GBP(£)
Greece	希腊	Europe Dollar	欧元	EUR(€)
Hungary	匈牙利	Forint	匈牙利福林	HUF
Iceland	冰岛	Icelandic Krona	冰岛克朗	ISK
Ireland	爱尔兰	Europe Dollar	欧元	EUR(€)
Italy	意大利	Europe Dollar	欧元	EUR(€)
Luxembourg	卢森堡	Europe Dollar	欧元	EUR(€)
Macedonia	马其顿	Denar	代纳尔	MKD
Malta	马耳他	Lira	马耳他里拉	MTL
Montenegro	黑山	Europe Dollar	欧元	EUR(€)
Netherlands	荷兰	Europe Dollar	欧元	EUR(€)
Norway	挪威	Krone	挪威克朗	NOK
Poland	波兰	Zloty	波兰兹罗提	PLN
Portugal	葡萄牙	Europe Dollar	欧元	EUR(€)
Romania	罗马尼亚	Leu	罗马尼亚列伊	ROL
Serbia	塞尔维亚	Serbia Dinar	塞尔维亚第纳尔	CSD
Slovak	斯洛伐克	Koruna	斯洛伐克克朗	SKK
Slovenia	斯洛文尼亚	Europe Dollar	欧元	EUR(€)
Spain	西班牙	Europe Dollar	欧元	EUR(€)
Sweden	瑞典	Krona	瑞典克朗	SEK
Switzerland	瑞士	Swiss Franc	瑞士法郎	CHF
Turkey	土耳其	Turkish Lira	土耳其里拉	TRY
Russia	俄罗斯	Ruble	卢布	RUB

美洲			
国家或地区		货币单位	缩写或符号
Argentina	阿根廷	Argentina Peso	阿根廷比索	ARS
Bolivia	玻利维亚	Boliviano	玻利维亚诺	BOB

续表

国家或地区		货币单位		缩写或符号
Brazil	巴　西	Real	巴西雷亚尔	BRL
Canada	加拿大	Canada Dollar	加拿大元	CAD
Chile	智　利	Chilean Peso	智利比索	CLP
Colombia	哥伦比亚	Colombian Peso	哥伦比亚比索	COU
Cuba	古　巴	Cuban Peso	古巴比索	CUC
Ecuaor	厄瓜多尔	Ecuadorian Sucre	厄瓜多尔苏克雷	ECS
Jamaica	牙买加	Jamaican Dollar	牙买加元	JMD
Mexico	墨西哥	Mexican Peso	墨西哥比索	MXN
Nicaragua	尼加拉瓜	Cordoba	尼加拉瓜科多巴	NIO
Panama	巴拿马	Panamanian Balboa	巴拿马巴波亚	PAB
Peru	秘　鲁	Nuevo Sol	新索尔	PEN
Trinidad & Tobago	特立尼达和多马哥	Trinidad and Tobago Dollar	特立尼达和多巴哥元	TT$
USA	美　国	Dollar	美元	USD($)
Uruguay	乌拉圭	New Uruguayan Peso	乌拉圭新比索	UYU
Venezuela	委内瑞拉	Venezuelan Bolivar	委内瑞拉博利瓦	VEB

非洲

国家或地区		货币单位		缩写或符号
Algeria	阿尔及利亚	Alerian Dinnar	阿尔及利亚第纳尔	AD
Angola	安哥拉	Kwanza	宽扎	AOA
Cameroon	喀麦隆	CFA-Franc	非洲金融共同体法郎	CFAF
Central African	中　非	CFA-Franc	非洲金融共同体法郎	CFAF
Chad	乍　得	CFA-Franc	非洲金融共同体法郎	CFAF
Congo	刚　果	CFA-Franc	非洲金融共同体法郎	CFAF
Egypt	埃　及	Egyptian Pounds	埃及镑	EGP
Ethiopia	埃塞俄比亚	Ethiopia Birr	埃塞俄比亚比尔	BTB
Gabon	加　蓬	CFA-Franc	非洲金融共同体法郎	CFAF
Ghana	加　纳	New Cedi	新塞地	GHC
Kenya	肯尼亚	Kenya Shilling	肯尼亚先令	KES
Ivory Coast	象牙海岸	CFA-Franc	非洲金融共同体法郎	CFAF
Liberia	利比里亚	Liberia Dollar	利比里亚元	LRD
Libya	利比亚	Libyan Dinar	利比亚第纳尔	LYD
Madagascar	马达加斯加	Malagasy ariary	马达加斯加阿里亚里	MGA
Mali	马　里	CFA-Franc	非洲金融共同体法郎	CFAF
Mauritania	毛里塔尼亚	Ouguiya	乌吉亚	MRO
Mauritius	毛里求斯	Mauritius Rupee	毛里求斯卢比	MUR
Morocco	摩洛哥	Dirham	摩洛哥迪拉姆	MAD
Niger	尼日尔	CFA-Franc	非洲金融共同体法郎	CFAF
Nigeria	尼日利亚	Naira	尼日利亚奈拉	NGN
Rwanda	卢旺达	Rwanda Franc	卢旺达法郎	RWF
Senegal	塞内加尔	CFA-Franc	非洲金融共同体法郎	CFA-FR

续表

国家或地区		货币单位		缩写或符号
Somalia	索马里	Somalian Shilling	索马里先令	SOS
South Africa	南　非	Rand	南非兰特	ZAR
Sudan	苏　丹	Sudanese Dinar	苏丹第纳尔	SDD
Tanzania	坦桑尼亚	Tanzanian Shilling	坦桑尼亚先令	TZS
Toto	多　哥	CFA-Franc	非洲金融共同体法郎	CFAF
Tunisia	突尼斯	Tunisian Dinar	突尼斯第纳尔	TND
Uganda	乌干达	Shilling	乌干达先令	UGX
Zambia	赞比亚	Kwacha	赞比亚克瓦查	ZMK

大洋洲

国家或地区		货币单位		缩写或符号
Australia	澳大利亚	Australian Dollar	澳大利亚元	AUD
Fiji	斐　济	Fiji Dollar	斐济元	FJD
New Zealand	新西兰	New Zealand Dollar	新西兰元	NZD

世界主要城市、机场三字代码
Main Cities and Codes

三字码	城市英文名	城市中文名	国家名称
AAL	AALBORG	奥尔堡	丹 麦
AAR	AARHUS	奥胡斯	丹 麦
ABJ	ABIDJAN	阿比让	科特迪瓦
ABZ	ABERDEEN	阿伯丁	英 国
ACC	ACCRA	阿克拉	加 纳
ADB	IZMIR	伊兹密尔	土耳其
ADD	ADDIS ABABA	亚的斯亚贝巴	埃塞俄比亚
ADL	ADELAIDE	阿德莱德	澳大利亚
AGB	AUGSBURG	奥格斯堡	德 国
AGP	MALAGA	马拉加	西班牙
AHO	ALGHERO	阿尔盖罗	意大利
AKL	AUCKLAND	奥克兰	新西兰
ALA	ALMATY	阿拉木图	哈萨克斯坦
ALC	ALICANTE	阿利坎特	西班牙
ALY	ALEXANDRIA	亚历山大港	埃 及
AMD	AHMEDABAD	艾哈迈达巴德	印 度
AMM	AMMAN	安曼	约 旦
AMS	AMSTERDAM	阿姆斯特丹	荷 兰
ANC	ANCHORAGE	安克雷奇	美 国
ANE	ANGERS	昂热	法 国
ANK	ANKARA	安卡拉	土耳其
ANR	ANTWERP	安特卫普	比利时
ASU	ASUNCION	亚松森	巴拉圭
ATH	ATHENS	雅典	希 腊
ATL	ATLANTA	亚特兰大	美 国
AUH	ABU DHABI	阿布扎比	阿联酋
BAH	BAHRAIN	巴林	巴 林
BAK	BAKU	巴库	阿塞拜疆
BCN	BARCELONA	巴塞罗那	西班牙
BDA	BERMUDA	百慕大	百慕大
BEG	BELGRADE	贝尔格莱德	南斯拉夫
BEL	BELEM	贝伦	巴 西
BER	BERLIN	柏林	德 国
BEY	BEIRUT	贝鲁特	黎巴嫩
BFS	BELFAST	贝尔法斯特	英 国
BGO	BERGEN	贝尔根	挪 威
BGW	BAGHDAD	巴格达	伊拉克

续表

三字码	城市英文名	城市中文名	国家名称
BHX	BIRMINGHAM	伯明翰	英　国
BIO	BILBAO	毕尔巴鄂	西班牙
BIQ	BIARRITZ	比亚里兹	法　国
BJL	BANJUL	班珠尔	冈比亚
BKK	BANGKOK	曼谷	泰　国
BKO	BAMAKO	巴马科	马　里
BLL	BILLUND	比隆	丹　麦
BLQ	BOLOGNA	博洛尼亚	意大利
BLR	BANGALORE	班加罗尔	印　度
BNE	BRISBANE	布里斯班	澳大利亚
BNJ	BONN	波恩	德　国
BOD	BORDEAUX	波尔多	法　国
BOG	BOGOTA	波哥大	哥伦比亚
BOM	BOMBAI	孟买	印　度
BOS	BOSTON	波士顿	美　国
BPN	BALIKPAPAN	巴厘巴板	印　尼
BRE	BREMEN	不来梅	德　国
BRN	BERNE	伯尔尼	瑞　士
BRS	BRISTOL	布里斯托尔	英　国
BRU	BRUSSELS	布鲁塞尔	比利时
BSB	BRASILIA	巴西利亚	巴　西
BSL	BASLE	巴塞尔	瑞　士
BTS	BRATISLAVA	布亚迪斯拉发	斯洛伐克
BTU	BINTULU	民都鲁	马来西亚
BUD	BUDAPEST	布达佩斯	匈牙利
BUE	BUENOS AIRES	布宜诺斯艾利斯	阿根廷
BUH	BUCHAREST	布加勒斯特	罗马尼亚
BWI	BALTIMOER	巴尔的摩	美　国
BWN	BANDAR SERI BEGAWAN	斯里巴加湾港	文　莱
BYU	BAYREUTH	拜罗伊特	德　国
BZV	BRAZZAVILLE	布拉柴维尔	刚　果
CAG	CAGLIARI	卡利亚里	意大利
CAI	CAIRO	开罗	埃　及
CAN	GUANGZHOU	广州	中　国
CAS	CASABLANCA	卡萨布兰卡	摩洛哥
CBR	CANBERRA	堪培拉	澳大利亚
CCS	CARACAS	加斯拉斯	委内瑞拉
CCU	CALCUTTA	加尔各达	印　度
CDG	PARIS-CHARLES DE GAULLE	巴黎戴高乐机场	法　国
CEB	CEBU	宿雾	菲律宾
CGK	JAKARTA Soekamo-Hatta Apt	雅加达	印　尼

续表

三字码	城市英文名	城市中文名	国家名称
CGN	COLOGNE	科隆	德国
CGO	ZHENGZHOU	郑州	中国
CGQ	CHANGCHUN	长春	中国
CHC	CHRISTCHURCH	基督堂市	新西兰
CHI	CHICAGO	芝加哥	美国
CJJ	CHUNG JU	青州	韩国
CJU	CHEJU	济州岛	韩国
CKG	CHONGQING	重庆	中国
CLE	CLEVELAND	克利夫兰	美国
CLT	CHARLOTTE	夏洛特	美国
CMB	COLOMBO	科伦坡	斯里兰卡
CMH	COLUMBUS	哥伦布	美国
CNS	CAIRNS	凯恩斯	澳大利亚
CNX	CHIANG MAI	清迈	泰国
CPH	COPENHAGEN	哥本哈根	丹麦
CPT	CAPE TOWN	开普敦	南非
CSX	CHANGSHA	长沙	中国
CTA	CATANIA	卡洛尼亚	意大利
CTU	CHENGDU	成都	中国
CVG	CINCINNATI	辛辛那提	美国
CWB	CURITIBA	库里蒂巴	巴西
DAC	DHAKA	达卡	孟加拉
DAM	DAMASCUS	大马士革	叙利亚
DAR	DAR ES SALAAM	达累斯萨拉姆	坦桑尼亚
DEL	DELHI	新德里	印度
DEN	DENVER	丹佛	美国
DFW	DALLAS	达拉斯	美国
DHA	DHAHRAN	宰赫兰	沙特阿拉伯
DKR	DAKAR	达喀尔	塞内加尔
DLA	DOUALA	杜阿拉	喀麦隆
DLC	DALIAN	大连	中国
DLU	DALI	大理	中国
DMM	DAMMAN	达曼	印度
DNH	DUNHUANG	敦煌	中国
DOH	DOHA	多哈	卡塔尔
DPS	DENPASAR	登巴萨/巴厘岛	印尼
DRS	DRESDEN	德累斯顿	德国
DRW	DARWIN	达尔文港	澳大利亚
DTM	DORTMUND	多特蒙德	德国
DTW	DETROIT	底特律	美国

续表

三字码	城市英文名	城市中文名	国家名称
DUB	DUBLIN	都柏林	爱尔兰
DUR	DURBAN	德班	南非
DUS	DUSSELDORF	杜塞尔多夫	德国
DXB	DUBAI	迪拜	阿联酋
DYG	ZHANGJIAJIE	张家界	中国
EBB	ENTEBBE	恩德培	乌干达
EDI	EDINBURGH	爱丁堡	英国
EIN	EINDHOVEN	埃因霍温	荷兰
EMA	NOTTINGHAM	诺丁汉	英国
ESB	ANKARA ESENBOGA	安卡拉	土耳其
EVN	YEREVAN	埃里温	亚美尼亚
EWR	NEW YORK/NEWARK	纽约/纽瓦克	美国
EZE	BUENOS AIRES	布宜诺斯艾利斯	阿根廷
FAO	FARO	法鲁	葡萄牙
FBU	OSLO	奥斯陆	挪威
FDH	FRIEDRICHSHAFEN	菲特烈	德国
FIH	KINSHASA	金沙萨	扎伊尔
FKS	FUKUSHIMA	福岛	日本
FLN	FLORIANOPOLIS	弗洛里亚诺波利斯	巴西
FLR	FLORENCE	佛罗伦萨	意大利
FMO	MUNSTER	明斯特	德国
FNA	FREETOWN	弗里敦	塞拉利昂
FNJ	PYONGYANG	平壤	朝鲜
FOC	FUZHOU	福州	中国
FOR	FORTALEZA	福塔莱萨	巴西
FRA	FARNKFURT	法兰克福	法国
FUK	FUKUOKA	福冈	日本
GBE	GABORONE	哈博罗内	博茨瓦纳
GCI	GUERNSEY	根西岛	英国
GDN	GDANSK	格但斯克	波兰
GIB	GIBRALTAR	直布罗陀	英国
GLA	GLASGOW	格拉斯哥	英国
GOA	GENOA	热那亚	意大利
GOT	GOTHENBURG	歌德堡	瑞典
GRU	SAO PAULO	圣保罗	巴西
GRZ	GRAZ	格拉茨	奥地利
GUM	GUAM	关岛	日本
GVA	GENEVA	日内瓦	瑞士
HAH	MORONI	摩朗尼	科摩罗
HAJ	HANOVER	汉诺威	德国

续表

三字码	城市英文名	城市中文名	国家名称
HAK	HAIKOU	海口	中国
HAM	HAMBURG	汉堡	德国
HAN	HANIO	河内	越南
HBA	HOBART	霍巴特	澳大利亚
HDY	HAT YAI	合艾	泰国
HEL	HELSINKI	赫尔辛基	芬兰
HET	HOHHOT	呼和浩特	中国
HFE	HEFEI	合肥	中国
HGH	HANGZHOU	杭州	中国
HHA	CHANGSHA	长沙	中国
HIJ	HIROSHIMA	广岛	日本
HKG	HONGKONG	香港	中国
HKT	PHUKET	普吉	泰国
HLD	HAILAR	海拉尔	中国
HLH	ULANHOT	乌兰浩特	中国
HNL	HONOLULU	檀香山	美国
HRB	HARBN	哈尔滨	中国
HRE	HARARE	哈拉雷	津巴布韦
HTA	CHITA	赤塔	俄罗斯
HTI	HAMILTON ISLAND	汉密尔顿岛	澳大利亚
HTN	HOTAN	和田	中国
IAH	HOUSTON	休斯敦	美国
ICN	INCHEON	仁川	韩国
IEV	KIEV	基辅	乌克兰
IKT	IRKUTSK	伊尔库次克	俄罗斯
INN	INNSBRUCK	因斯布鲁克	奥地利
IPH	IPOH	怡保	马来西亚
ISB	ISAMABAD	伊斯兰堡	巴基斯坦
IST	ISTANBUL	伊斯坦布尔	土耳其
IZM	IZMIR	伊兹密尔	土耳其
JED	JEDDAH	吉达	沙特阿拉伯
JER	JERSEY	泽西岛	英国
JFK	NEW YORK	纽约	美国
JHB	JOHOR BAHRU	柔拂州	马来西亚
JHG	XISHUANGBANNA	景洪	中国
JIB	DJIBOUTI	吉布提	吉布提
JKT	JAKARTA	雅加达	印尼
JNB	JOHANNESBURG	约翰内斯堡	南非
JOG	YOGYAKARTA	日惹	印尼
KAN	KANO	卡诺	尼日利亚

续表

三字码	城市英文名	城市中文名	国家名称
KBL	KABUL	喀布尔	阿富汗
KBP	KIEV	基辅	乌克兰
KCH	KUCHING	古晋	马来西亚
KEF	REYKJAVIK	雷克雅未克	冰 岛
KEL	KIEL	基尔	德 国
KHH	KAOHSIUNG	高雄	中 国
KHI	KARACHI	卡拉奇	巴基斯坦
KHV	KHABAROVSK	哈巴罗夫斯克	俄罗斯
KIJ	NIIGATA	新潟	日 本
KIN	KINGSTON	金斯敦	牙买加
KIX	OSAKA	大阪	日 本
KLU	KLAGENFURT	克拉根福	奥地利
KOA	KONA	科纳	美 国
KOJ	KAGOSHIMA	鹿儿岛	日 本
KRK	KRAKOW	克拉科夫	波 兰
KRL	KORLA	库尔勒	中 国
KRT	KHARTOUM	喀土穆	苏 丹
KRY	KARAMAY	克拉玛依	中 国
KTM	KATHMANDU	加德满都	尼泊尔
KTW	KATOWICE	卡托维兹	波 兰
KUA	KUANTAN	关丹	马来西亚
KUF	SAMARA	萨马拉	俄罗斯
KUL	KUALA-LUMPUR	吉隆坡	马来西亚
KWI	KUWAIT	科威特	科威特
LAS	LAS VEGAS	拉斯维加斯	美 国
LAX	LOS ANGELES	洛杉矶	美 国
LBA	LEEDS/BRADFORO	利兹	英 国
LBV	LIBREVILLE	利伯维尔	加 蓬
LCA	LARNACA	拉纳卡	塞浦路斯
LDU	LAHAD DATU	拿笃	马来西亚
LED	ST. PETERSBURG	圣彼得堡	俄罗斯
LEJ	LEIPZIG/HALLE	莱比锡	德 国
LGA	NEW YORK-LE GUARDIA	纽约-拉瓜地	美 国
LGK	LANGKAWI	兰卡威	马来西亚
LHE	LAHORE	拉合尔	巴基斯坦
LHR	LONDON-HEATHROW	伦敦-希思罗	英 国
LIL	LILLE	里尔	法 国
LIM	LIMA	利马	秘 鲁
LIN	MILAN LINATE	米兰-利纳特	意大利
LIS	LISBON	里斯本	葡萄牙
LJU	LJUBLJANA	卢布尔雅那	斯洛文尼亚

续表

三字码	城市英文名	城市中文名	国家名称
LNZ	LINZ	林茨	奥地利
LOS	LAGOS	拉各斯	尼日利亚
LPB	LAPAZ	拉巴斯	玻利维亚
LPL	LIVERPOOL	利物浦	英国
LUG	LUGANO	卢加诺	瑞士
LUN	LUSAKA	卢萨卡	赞比亚
LUX	LUXEMBOURG	卢森堡	卢森堡
LXA	LHASA	拉萨	中国
LYS	LYON	里昂	法国
MAA	MADRAS	马德拉斯	印度
MAD	MADRID	马德里	西班牙
MAO	MANAUS	马瑙斯	巴西
MAN	MANCHESTER	曼彻斯特	英国
MCI	KANSAS CITY	堪萨斯城	美国
MCO	ORLANDO	奥兰多	美国
MCT	MUSCAT	马斯喀特	阿曼
MEL	MELBOURNE	墨尔本	澳大利亚
MEM	MEMPHIS	孟菲斯	美国
MES	MEDAN	棉兰	印尼
MEX	MEXICO CITY	墨西哥城	墨西哥
MFM	MACAU	澳门	中国
MIA	MIAMI	迈阿密	美国
MIL	MILAN	米兰	意大利
MLA	MALTA	马耳他	马耳他
MLE	MALE	马累	马尔代夫
MMA	MALMO	马尔默	瑞典
MNL	MANILA	马尼拉	菲律宾
MOW	MOSCOW	莫斯科	俄罗斯
MPL	MONTPELLIER	蒙彼利埃	法国
MRS	MARSEILLE	马赛	法国
MRU	MAURITIUS	毛里求斯	毛里求斯
MSP	MINNEAPOLIS-ST PAUL	明尼阿波利斯-圣保罗机场	美国
MSQ	MINSK	明斯克	白俄罗斯
MSY	NEW ORLEANS	新奥尔良	美国
MTY	MONTERREY	蒙特雷	墨西哥
MUC	MUNICH	慕尼黑	德国
MVD	MONTEVIDEO	蒙得维的亚	乌拉圭
MXP	MILAN MALPENSA	米兰,马尔本萨	意大利
MYJ	MATSUYAMA	松山	日本
NAP	NAPLES	那不勒斯	意大利
NAT	NATAL	纳塔尔	巴西

续表

三字码	城市英文名	城市中文名	国家名称
NBO	NAIROBI	内罗毕	肯尼亚
NCE	NICE	尼斯	法国
NCL	NEWCASTLE	纽卡斯尔	英国
NGS	NAGASAKI	长崎	日本
NNG	NANNING	南宁	中国
NKG	NANJING	南京	中国
NOU	NOUMEA	努美阿	新喀里多尼亚
NQY	NEWQUAY	纽基	英国
NRK	NORRKOPING	诺尔雪平	瑞典
NRT	TOKYO	东京	日本
NTE	NANTES	南特	法国
NUE	NUREMBERG	纽伦堡	德国
NYC	NEW YORK	纽约	美国
ODS	ODESSA	敖德萨	乌克兰
OKA	OKINAWA	冲绳	日本
OKJ	OKAYAMA	冈山	日本
OOL	GOLD COAST	黄金海岸	澳大利亚
OPO	PORTO	波尔图	葡萄牙
ORD	CHICAGO	芝加哥	美国
OSA	OSAKA	大阪	日本
OSL	OSLO	奥斯陆	挪威
OVB	NOVOSIBIRSK	新西伯利亚	俄罗斯
PAD	PADERBORN	帕德博恩	德国
PDX	PORTLAND	波特兰	美国
PEK	BEIJING	北京	中国
PEN	PENANG	槟城	马来西亚
PER	PERTH	珀斯	澳大利亚
PHL	PHILADELPHIA	费城	美国
PHX	PHOENIX	凤凰城	美国
PLH	PLYMOUTH	普利茅斯	英国
PLM	PALEMBANG	巨港	印尼
PLZ	PORT ELIZABETH	伊丽莎白港	南非
PMI	PALMA DE MALLORCA	帕尔马	西班牙
PMO	PALERMO	巴勒莫	意大利
PNH	PHNOM PENH	金边	柬埔寨
POM	PORT MORESBY	莫勒斯比港	巴布亚新几内亚
POZ	POZNAN	波兹南	波兰
PRG	PRAGUE	布拉格	捷克
PSA	PISA	比萨	意大利
PUF	PAU	波城	法国
PUS	PUSAN	釜山	韩国

续表

三字码	城市英文名	城市中文名	国家名称
PVG	SHANGHAI PUDONG	上海浦东	中　国
REC	RECIFE	累西腓	巴　西
REG	REGGIO CALABRIA	雷焦卡拉布里亚	意大利
RGN	YANGON	仰光	缅　甸
RIO	RIO DE JANEIRO	里约热内卢	巴　西
RIX	RIGA	里加	拉脱维亚
ROB	MONROVIA	蒙罗维亚	利比里亚
ROM(FCO)	ROME	罗马	意大利
RTM	ROTTERDAM	鹿特丹	荷　兰
RUH	RIYADH	利雅得	沙特阿拉伯
SAH	SANAA	萨那	也　门
SAN	SAN DIEGO	圣地亚哥	美　国
SAO	SAO PAULO	圣保罗	巴　西
SBW	SIBU	泗务	马来西亚
SCL	SANTIAGO	圣地亚哥	智　利
SDF	LOUISVILLE	路易斯维尔	美　国
SDJ	SENDAI	仙台	日　本
SDK	SANDAKAN	山打根	马来西亚
SEA	SEATTLE	西雅图	美　国
SEL	SEOUL	首尔	韩　国
SFO	SAN FRANCISCO	旧金山	美　国
SFS	SUBIC BAHIA	苏比克湾	菲律宾
SGN	HO CHI MINH CITY	胡志明市	越　南
SHA	SHANGHAI	上海	中　国
SHE	SHENYANG	沈阳	中　国
SHJ	SHARJAH	沙迦	阿联酋
SIN	SINGAPORE	新加坡	新加坡
SJC	SAN JOSE	圣何塞	美　国
SJJ	SARAJEVO	萨拉热窝	南斯拉夫
SJW	SHIJIAZHUANG	石家庄	中　国
SKG	THESSALONIKI	萨洛尼卡	希　腊
SKP	SKOPJE	斯科普里	马其顿
SNN	SHANNON	香农	爱尔兰
SOF	SOFIA	索菲亚	保加利亚
SOU	SOUTHAMPTON	南安普敦	英　国
SPK	SAPPORO	札幌	日　本
SPN	SAIPAN	塞班岛	美　国
SPU	SPLIT	斯普里特	克罗地亚
SSA	SALVADOR	萨尔瓦多	巴　西
SSG	MALABO	马拉博	赤道几内亚

续表

三字码	城市英文名	城市中文名	国家名称
STL	SAINT LOUIS	圣路易斯	美国
STO	STOCKHOLM	斯德哥尔摩	瑞典
STR	STUTTGART	斯图加特	德国
SUB	SURABAYA	泗水	印尼
SVG	STAVANGER	斯塔万格	挪威
SVQ	SEVILLE	赛维利亚	西班牙
SVX	SVERDLOVSK	叶卡捷琳堡	俄罗斯
SXB	STRASBOURG	斯特拉斯堡	法国
SYD	SYDNEY	悉尼	澳大利亚
SYX	SANYA	三亚	中国
SYZ	SHIRAZ	设拉子	伊朗
SZG	SALZBURG	萨尔茨堡	奥地利
SZX	SHENZHEN	深圳	中国
SZZ	SZCZECIN	什切青	波兰
TAE	TAEGU	大丘	韩国
TAO	QINGDAO	青岛	中国
TAS	TASHKENT	塔什干	乌兹别克斯坦
TBS	TBILISI	第比利斯	格鲁吉亚
THR	TEHRAN	德黑兰	伊朗
TIA	TIRANA	地拉那	阿尔巴尼亚
TIP	TRIPOLI	的黎波里	利比亚
TLL	TALLINN	塔林	爱沙尼亚
TLS	TOULOUSE	图卢兹	法国
TLV	TEL AVIV	特拉维夫	以色列
TNA	JINAN	济南	中国
TOY	TOYOMA	富山	日本
TPA	TAMPA	坦帕	美国
TPE	TAIPEI	台北	中国
TRN	TURIN	都灵	意大利
TRS	TRIESTE	的里雅斯特	意大利
TSN	TIANJIN	天津	中国
TUN	TUNIS	突尼斯	突尼斯
TXL	BERLIN	柏林	德国
TYN	TAIYUAN	太原	中国
TYO	TOKYO	东京	日本
ULN	ULAN BATOR	乌兰巴托	蒙古
ULY	ULYANOVSK	乌里扬诺夫斯克	俄罗斯
URC	URUMQI	乌鲁木齐	中国
VCE	VENICE	威尼斯	意大利
VIE	VIENNA	维也纳	奥地利
VLC	VALENCIA	巴伦西亚	西班牙

续表

三字码	城市英文名	城市中文名	国家名称
VNO	VILNIUS	维尔纽斯	立陶宛
VRN	VERONA	维罗那	意大利
VVO	VLADIVOSTOK	符拉迪沃斯托克	俄罗斯
WAS	WASHINGTON	华盛顿	美国
WAW	WARSAW	华沙	波兰
WDH	WINDHOEK	温得和克	纳米比亚
WLG	WELLINGTON	惠灵顿	新西兰
WUH	WUHAN	武汉	中国
XIL	XILINHOT	锡林浩特	中国
XIY	XIAN	西安	中国
XMN	XIAMEN	厦门	中国
XNN	XINING	西宁	中国
YAO	YAOUNDE	雅温得	喀麦隆
YCD	NANAIMO	纳奈莫	加拿大
YEG	EDMONTON	埃德蒙顿	加拿大
YGK	KINGSTON	金斯敦	牙买加
YHZ	HALIFAX	哈利法克斯	加拿大
YLW	KELOWNA	基洛纳	加拿大
YMQ(YUL)	MONTREAL	蒙特利尔	加拿大
YOW	OTTAWA	渥太华	加拿大
YQB	QUEBEC	魁比克	加拿大
YQG	WINDSOR	温莎	加拿大
YQR	REGINA	里贾纳	加拿大
YVR	VANCOUVER	温哥华	加拿大
YWG	WINNIPEG	温尼伯	加拿大
YWH	VICTORIA-INNER HARBOUR	维多利亚港	加拿大
YXU	LONDON	伦敦	英国
YXY	WHITEHORSE	怀特霍斯	加拿大
YYC	CALGARY	卡尔加里	加拿大
YYJ	VICTORIA	维多利亚	加拿大
YYZ(YTO)	TORONTO	多伦多	加拿大
ZAG	ZAGREB	萨格勒布	克罗地亚
ZNZ	ZANZIBAR	桑吉巴尔	坦桑尼亚
ZRH	ZURICH	苏黎世	瑞士
ZUH	ZHUHAI	珠海	中国

《民航地勤英语》(第二版)

尊敬的老师:

您好!

为了方便您更好地使用本教材,获得最佳教学效果,我们特向使用该书作为教材的教师赠送本教材配套参考资料。如有需要,请完整填写"教师联系表"并加盖所在单位系(院)公章,免费向出版社索取。

北京大学出版社

教 师 联 系 表

教材名称	《民航地勤英语》(第二版)		
姓名:	性别:	职务:	职称:
E-mail:	联系电话:		邮政编码:
供职学校:		所在院系:	
			(章)
学校地址:			
教学科目与年级:		班级人数:	
通信地址:			

填写完毕后,请将此表邮寄给我们,我们将为您免费寄送本教材配套资料,谢谢!

北京市海淀区成府路205号
北京大学出版社外语编辑部　郝妮娜　　邮 购 部 电话:010-62534449
邮政编码:100871　　　　　　　　　　市场营销部电话:010-62750672
电子邮箱:bdhnn2011@126.com　　　　外语编辑部电话:010-62759634